JEFF G

GEN SeXYZ

Love

Sexuality

& Youth

WHITAKER
HOUSE

Unless otherwise indicated, all Scripture quotations are taken from *The Message: The Bible in Contemporary Language* by Eugene H. Peterson, © 1993, 1994, 1995, 1996, 2000, 2001, 2002. Used by permission of NavPress Publishing Group. All rights reserved. Represented by Tyndale House Publishers, Inc. Scripture quotations marked (GNT) are taken from the Good News Translation – Second Edition, © 1992 by the American Bible Society. Used by permission. Scripture quotations marked (NASB) are taken from the updated *New American Standard Bible®*, NASB®, © 1960, 1971, 1977, 1995, 2020 by The Lockman Foundation. All rights reserved. Used by permission. (www.Lockman.org).

Boldface type in the Scripture quotations indicates the author's emphasis.

GEN SEXYZ
Love, Sexuality & Youth

www.ythology.com
511 South 4th St.
Minneapolis, MN 55415
616.638.6854
jeffgrenell@ythology.com

ISBN: 978-1-64123-587-7
eBook ISBN: 978-1-64123-586-0
Printed in the United States of America

© 2021 by Jeff Grenell

Whitaker House
1030 Hunt Valley Circle
New Kensington, PA 15068
www.whitakerhouse.com

Library of Congress Cataloging-in-Publication Data (Pending)

1 2 3 4 5 6 7 8 9 10 11 **W** 28 27 26 25 24 23 22 21

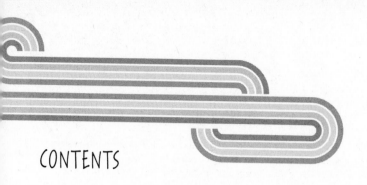

CONTENTS

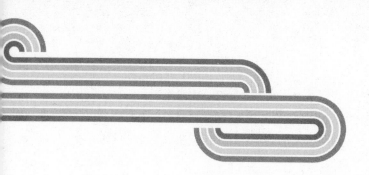

If I speak with human eloquence and angelic ecstasy but don't love,

I'm nothing but the creaking of a rusty gate.

If I speak God's Word with power, revealing all his mysteries and making everything plain as day, and if I have faith that says to a mountain, "Jump," and it jumps,

but I don't love, I'm nothing.

If I give everything I own to the poor and even go to the stake to be burned as a martyr, but I don't love, I've gotten nowhere. So, no matter what I say, what I believe, and what I do,

I'm bankrupt without love.

Love never gives up.
Love cares more for others than for self.
Love doesn't want what it doesn't have.
Love doesn't strut,
Doesn't have a swelled head,
Doesn't force itself on others,
Isn't always "me first,"
Doesn't fly off the handle,
Doesn't keep score of the sins of others,

Doesn't revel when others grovel,
Takes pleasure in the flowering of truth,
Puts up with anything,
Trusts God always,
Always looks for the best,
Never looks back,
But keeps going to the end.

Love never dies. Inspired speech will be over some day; praying in tongues will end; understanding will reach its limit. We know only a portion of the truth, and what we say about God is always incomplete. But when the Complete arrives, our incompletes will be canceled.

When I was an infant at my mother's breast, I gurgled and cooed like any infant. When I grew up, I left those infant ways for good.

We don't yet see things clearly. We're squinting in a fog, peering through a mist. But it won't be long before the weather clears and the sun shines bright! We'll see it all then, see it all as clearly as God sees us, knowing him directly just as he knows us!

But for right now, until that completeness, we have three things to do to lead us toward that consummation: Trust steadily in God, hope unswervingly, love extravagantly.

And the best of the three is love.

—1 Corinthians 13

Corrupt the young. Get them away from religion. Encourage their interest in sex. Make them superficial by focusing their attention on sports, sensual entertainments, and trivialities. By specious argument cause the breakdown of the old moral virtues: honesty, sobriety, and self-restraint.

          —Vladimir Lenin, 1921, *How to Destroy the West*

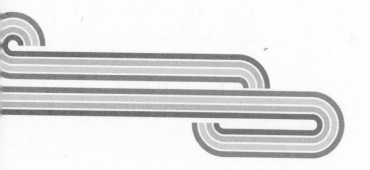

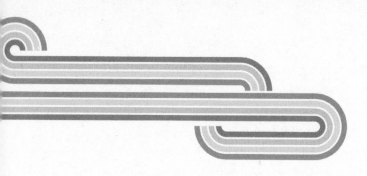

PREFACE

Corrupt the young. Check. Gen Z has a 4 percent biblical worldview.
Get them away from religion. Check. Only 25 percent of Gen Z sees
attending church as "very important." *Encourage their interest in
sex.* Check. *Cause the breakdown of the old moral virtues like honesty,
sobriety, and self-restraint.* Check.

We could go on through each of these prophetic statements from
Lenin in 1921 and see why America is where it is today.

XYZ

Just look at the title of this book. This project is a compilation of the
sexuality handoff from Generation X (the adult parents of young
people today), to Generation Y (the Millennials), and finally to
Generation Z (teenagers and early twenty-somethings). We can learn
a lot from this generational handoff—mostly that it has failed to
pass the Christian faith along to the following generation.

The narrative throughout this book is a clear picture of how we have
gotten here as a nation: by abandoning God as the center of our lives
in the past few generations. And while we will do some commentary
about Generation X and their influence upon our society, most of this

study is about the Generation Y/Millennial and the Generation Z young people in America.

> *What is clear is that the biblical picture of Psalm 78 and the plans for an intended handoff of the faith, the works, and the miracles of God from one generation to the next is not happening in twenty-first century America.*

To be clear, Generation X was born about 1960 through 1980, although every sociological model will vary by a few years at the beginning and the end of a generational set. The Generation Y or the Millennial set was born around 1980 through 1998, as most sociological models will state. Finally, Generation Z was born around 1998 through 2013. Of interest to all of us is the naming of the next generation to follow. Some have dubbed them Alpha Gen, Like Generation, and even Generation A.

I want my relationship with my husband to be just like my mom and dad's.
—Halley, age 16

Let's try and understand the present teenagers and young adults in America today. Gen Z counts sexuality as more important than friends, family, and their faith.[1] In the Barna Group's newest research on teens' top guides for moral issues, youth pastors or spiritual leaders do not even make the top ten! Cable news, Google, and YouTube are sought out before a youth leader or spiritual leader.[2]

Unfortunately, this is where we are today.

---

1. Barna Group, *Gen Z: The Culture, Beliefs and Motivations Shaping the Next Generation* (Carol Stream, IL: Tyndale House, 2018).
2. Barna Group, *Barna Trends 2018: What's New and What's Next at the Intersection of Faith and Culture* (Grand Rapids, MI: Baker Books, 2017).

America today is experiencing another revolution. The most recent transformation of America began during the time of the religious awakening called the Jesus movement in the late 1960s, and the resulting sexual revolution that arose out of that awakening in the following twenty-five years up until the 1990s. What began as the church's greatest hour following the Jesus movement turned quickly as the sexual revolution took over. And the church has never recovered.

When the church lost love, the church lost the argument.

We are all looking for l. o. v. e.
—Reggie Dabbs, youth communicator

BOXES

I know it is popular to get out of the box and break traditions. This book will contend that, actually, what we all really like *is a box*. A set of standards or a way to view everything. To be honest, people who try to break out of the box, or traditions, end up creating new ones to replace the old ones anyway. A new box.

By writing a book on love, sexuality, and youth, I have spent a lot of time in research and relationship. I've taken several introductions from a variety of books I have read on the subject of sexuality and come up with a common paraphrased beginning of just about every book written on sexuality. A *box* or framework authors operate out of.

Right now, as I write this book, there are six books on the topic of sexuality on my table. Seemingly everyone who has ever written from a religious approach on this topic of sexuality, almost without exception, begins with the following kind of statement:

> I want to look at the intent of the Scriptures in an unbiased way, as true as I can, and from both sides of the argument, because I have personal experience with this topic.

Even given this commitment, there are two or three different conclusions within the six books in front of me. This little paraphrase regarding the handling of this topic has come from those who are writing from a *classic* and conservative approach to Scripture, from those who are writing from an *emerging* and progressive approach to Scripture, and from those who are writing from a *secular* approach who are much more cultural in their thinking.

It really is funny that some of the most brilliant minds who have written on the topic of sexuality have begun with somewhat the same comment.

Additionally, it is not just the *beginnings* of these books on sexuality that sound so familiar. It really is funny that some of the most brilliant minds who have written on this topic of sexuality have *ended* on somewhat the same finding. Parenthetically, yes, there are extremists who run off from each end of the argument. But there is no value in listening to them.

However, looking at the same authors and the introductions to so many books I've read, here is a paraphrased statement of the intended conclusion of almost every writer:

> No matter our differences, we should all love and accept each other in the end.

A popular default approach and statement. For good reason. It can also be said that some of the most brilliant minds who have written on the topic of sexuality basically are standing in two simple *boxes*. Let me pare the argument down into two boxes.

The first box is the classic or conservative approach that claims sexuality is clear in Scripture. They say the sexual revolution going on in America today—with regard to sexual identity issues of gender, the sanctity of marriage, and sexual immorality—is part of the sexual disorder or prohibition contrary to clearly stated biblical principles we will talk about throughout this book.

> *The scriptural principles for the first box are found in the words of Moses in the book of Genesis, Solomon in Proverbs, Jesus in Matthew, Paul in Romans and other texts, Jude in the book of Jude, and John in Revelation. In these and other texts, we have principles defining the sanctity of humankind as male and female, the sanctity of marriage between a man and a woman, and the sanctity of romantic and sexual relationships between a man and woman within marriage.*

The second box is the emerging or progressive approach that claims sexuality is not so clear in Scripture. They say the sexual revolution going on in America today with regard to sexual identity issues of gender, the sanctity of marriage, and sexual immorality is part of the rediscovery and evolution of sexuality because Scripture isn't speaking about the same sexual phenomenon that exists in our contemporary life.

> *The principles for the second box are also found in some of these same Scriptures and also in subjective moral reasoning from culture and personal feelings.*

The brightest minds in history in both of these boxes have thought upon and written conclusively on the subject of sexuality. I'm sure many of the authors who have written on this topic feel like they have added something unique to the discussion. I daresay everything has been said on this topic. But let me add my thoughts from another perspective.

I don't even want to hear about sexuality conversations anymore if they aren't accompanied with love.
—Genesis, age 20

A LOVE REVOLUTION

When the church lost love, the church lost the argument.

I want to look at the intent of the Scriptures in an unbiased way, as true as I can, and from both sides of the argument, because I have personal experience with this topic. My youngest brother is gay. Aside from my study and research, I have the personal relational experience of a gay brother. And within this family setting, we have had to navigate our scriptural and relational ethic. To walk in both truth and grace. Love and holiness. Our family, including my brother and his partner, hold tightly to our theology *and our relationship!* Even though we may disagree with each other in our sexuality ethic.

Too many people have lost the right to even be in the conversation or the argument because *they have lost the love.* We do not have to shed our principles or ethics at the door of relationship. We must all have an understanding that we can agree to disagree. Just like our family had to do, or your family has to do, or our society must do. We all must meet the sexual revolution face to face with a love revolution.

There are really two main reasons I am writing on this topic:

First, *to promote a love revolution.* An uprising of Christians who understand the times and know what to do. Similar to the sons of Issachar, one of the tribes of Israel in the Old Testament. Moses says from the tribe of Issachar came *"men who understood both the times and Israel's duties"* (1 Chronicles 12:32). They also had over two hundred captains who led the people. This is a remarkable tribe. We must take this valuable characteristic trait to heart: that we would understand the times we are living in and know what to do about them.

I believe the church should be like the sons of Issachar. Looking at the times and the conditions of sexuality in our society, the church should be standing alongside of the sexual revolution with its own overwhelming tsunami of love. Instead of holding up our fist like the proverbial ant in front of the train to this crashing wave on the shores of America.

Second, *to promote a holiness revolution*. I am writing for the people who may have never heard the biblical narratives on sexuality and for those who might need to unlearn some things about sexuality. The younger generations in the Millennial and Gen Z sets have never seen the church as lovers—they have seen the church as haters. I believe you can hold strongly to truth and grace at the same time! The church does not have to shed its truth at the door of relationship.

It is no secret, and you will see it throughout multiple studies, that Gen Z has the lowest biblical worldview of any generational set in American history and lacks a Christian ethic of unbelievable proportions. Meaning they have joined the conversation and met the argument head-on with love...but not with truth.

The church should have met the sexual revolution with *a love and truth revolution* twenty-five years ago. To hang on tightly to both truth and love. This kind of ethic would have made a huge difference in the sexual relationships of teenagers, human trafficking, marriage, gender theology, women equality rights, and the relationship between the church and the LGBTQ+ community.

> If my friends see that I love them,
> I can talk to them about anything then.
> —James, age 13

FINALLY

Love is the great equalizer in our relationships. Given the moment our youth culture is in right now, it is important that we define and redefine love and sexuality, and how they relate to youth. But it is just as important that we teach young people how to communicate with each other about their differences. You will see there is a demand in this book. This book demands that the greatest impact a generation could have on their contemporaries is to help solve the worst of its problems. Christian young people need to understand their influence on their friends is dependent on love and truth.

The problems in the youth culture today are many—including the broken family, spiraling theological literacy, self-harm, depression and mental health, identity, social media, and the sexual revolution. If the greatest impact a generation could have on their contemporaries is to help solve the worst of its problems, then we will choose sexuality for this project.

One important thing to keep in mind throughout this book are *my* expectations. Let me explain....

I cannot tell you how many times young people have told me they can handle the deeper things of God. Often, teenagers have told me, "Give me more, I can handle it." *Do not underestimate how much a teenager can comprehend. On any subject.* So, like my approach in thirty-six years of youth ministry, this will not be childish or shallow or filled with Nickelodeon language. It will be childlike and mature and truthful.

To deal with the topic of sexuality and youth requires that we understand completely God's love *and* truth. His love is the grace of relationship and how we *behave* in the argument; His truth is the holiness of sexuality and what we *believe* in the argument. I have watched far too many discussions on this topic turn into arguments and, ultimately, anger—and then hatred. Hopefully, by the end of this book, we can all say we have understood and loved a little more.

I was recently walking out of my church in downtown Minneapolis on a Sunday afternoon during the Gay and Lesbian Pride Weekend. As I walked out of the church with several of my friends, a crowd of about fifty or so people were yelling at us and shoving signs in our faces and calling us bigots and haters. I understand that not every gay and lesbian person or group is this way. But this crowd was angry. I'm sure some of them for good reason.

Most of the church crowd I was with just simply walked away and did not respond. But I'm comfortable in this setting and walked over to a person with a megaphone who was leading the crowd. He sneered at me, and I introduced myself.

When I told him my name, he was shocked. Obviously, he knew my gay brother. He put the megaphone down and told the people around him that I was Ric Grenell's brother. I've gotten used to being famous for being my little brother's brother. It comes with the territory when your brother is an established political figure globally and you're just an evangelical preacher.

As the crowd became a little less noisy, I turned to the man and five or ten of his friends and I said, "Let me ask you a question. Who is yelling and angry here? Not me and my church friends. There is no one here who hates you. I'm not sure what you think about the church, but this one doesn't hate you and we are not angry. Or yelling at you. You are hating on us and you are yelling at us." He quieted down and after a short conversation, he thanked me for being civil.

Walking back to my condo in downtown Minneapolis that afternoon, I was broken. And burdened again for the church in America. I was burdened for whatever hate the church has caused in this argument and our relationship with the LBGTQ+ community. I was burdened to make sure that I continued to play a healing role in this narrative. Because I resolved many years ago to commit to a very important ethic that I have tried to keep throughout my life.

That I never want to win an argument and lose a friendship. And so we begin with love.

Jeff Grenell
Ythology

I grew up in a much more conservative time. I was raised in a typical Puritan Midwestern Methodist home and there was a lot of hurt and hypocrisy in those times. And I think that whatever part Playboy played and that I managed to play in terms of the sexual revolution came out of what I saw in the negative part of that life and tried to change things in some positive way so that people could choose, you know, alternate personal ways of living their lives.[3]   —Hugh Hefner

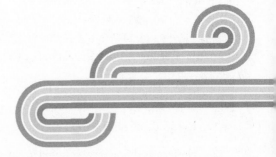

3. Jane Skinner with John Gibson, "Hugh Hefner Reflects on Turning 80," *Fox News*, April 6, 2006 (https://www.foxnews.com/story/hugh-hefner-reflects-on-turning-80.amp).

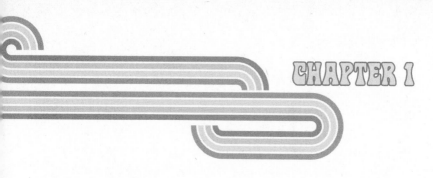

CHAPTER 1

THE DEVIL STOLE SEX

The Sexual Revolution

The devil knows he cannot steal God from us. So, he stole the next most important thing from us. The devil stole love from us. And when the devil stole love from us, he stole sex. See, when love is removed from sexuality, then we get a dangerous and new counterfeit for sexuality. One that is defined by a loveless sexual revolution.

Before we get into the sexual revolution, let me give you a quick definition of both *sexuality* and *revolution* so we can all be on the same page as we begin. We will deal with a complete spiritual and *theological* perspective of sexuality in the next chapter, but let's look over a more natural *teleological* definition of these terms first.

TELEOLOGY

Teleology is the understanding of why something exists. It is the foundational study of the natural purpose of something.

The *Merriam-Webster Dictionary* defines teleology the following way:

1. the study of evidences of design in nature

2. the fact or character attributed to nature or natural processes of being directed toward an end or shaped by a purpose

3.   the use of design or purpose as an explanation of natural
     phenomena

Using teleology, do you see the important concepts in the definition
of sexuality? The *design*, the *nature*, and the *purpose* of sexuality are
all part of understanding our subject for this book. We will see the
spiritual in the second chapter, but there is an important *natural* design
of sexuality also. Sexuality is a broad topic. You will see in each of the
definitions that sexuality spans science, biology, human conception,
birth, gender, identity, human relations, and behavior or promiscuity.

> We have reduced sexuality to physiological feelings,
> urges, and thoughts. Its essence, however, is spiritual.
> —Heath Adamson, global director, Next Generation Commission

SEXUALITY

Let's look at sexuality. Here are several definitions for sexuality as we
begin this journey.

> The quality or state of being sexual: the condition of having
> sex, sexual activity, expression of sexual receptivity or inter-
> est especially when excessive   —*Merriam-Webster*

> The quality of being sexual, especially sexual orientation and
> behavior   —*The Free Dictionary*

> The capacity for sexual feelings   —*Oxford Dictionary*

> Sexuality is just one of those things you are born with, you do
> not choose it, it's just part of who you are.
>   —*Urban Dictionary*

The importance of the teleological definition of sexuality
suggests there is a complementary and natural use of sexuality.

You could combine the definitions and come up with: *"the sexual expression and behavioral feelings that you are born with."* Quite an interesting summation from those dictionaries. Basically, sexuality is comprehensive in this discussion and entails a spectrum of topics *because sexuality is wide-reaching.*

Which brings us to the definition of a revolution.

REVOLUTION

You may have heard of the cultural revolution and the American Revolution and the French Revolution, or certain other global revolutions. But the sexual revolution we are going through now is just as real.

The teleology of a revolution is interesting. The compilation of its definitions means a *radical turnaround*, *dramatic wide-reaching overthrow*, *grand change*, or *replacement of something with another.*

When a revolution is underway, it brings not only change to the government and structure of a nation, it also brings change to its society and ultimately its people. A revolution could be a radical change in society's codes, language, and morality. Often, these changes take place from events or a movement that gains power.

What we've seen in the last twenty-five years in America is a swift change because of the influence of the information and technology age. From the political, sociological, entertainment, corporate, educational, household/family, and religious settings, we have seen sweeping changes reshape the landscape of our nation—ultimately the world. When you place sexuality and revolution together, you can see how impactful this can be.

WHAT IS A SEXUAL REVOLUTION?

One of the cultural realities of the Millennial and Gen Z sets is that they are living in a real and historic sexual revolution. Maybe the most staggering society-shifting tsunami to ever hit the shores of youth. The effects of this revolution are undeniable. It is true America has gone through several sexual revolutions. But *this* one that the Millennial and Gen Z sets are growing up in now is undoubtedly epic in its impact.

As has happened in the wake of other sexual revolutions, the response of a generation to the onslaught of such a revolution remains to be seen. But right now, the sexual revolution is winning the war on youth in the twenty-first century.

A sexual revolution changes thought, language, and behavior. Look at it this way.

> *A sexual revolution changes* **thought** *through overwhelming comprehensive counterculture. A sexual revolution changes* **language** *by challenging classic definitions with emerging language definitions. A sexual revolution then changes* **behavior** *by changing thought and language. It really is chilling to see radical shifts in thought, language, and behavior as we see today.*

Every generation has had a revolution of sexuality of some kind. It is not germane to the Millennial or the Gen Z sets. There have been changes in every culture because of sexuality. From the way people *think* to the way they *dress*. We've seen the historic *burning of the bra*, the *student movement* in the 1960s, the *Jesus Movement* in the 1970s, *the Pill*, *rap music*, the *loss of censorship* in the movies, the rising *acceptance of homosexuality* in the 1990s, the *Federal Marriage Amendment* of 2002 through 2015, and the proliferation of *sex and hookups on mobile devices*.

Today in America, maybe the most astounding and dramatic movement or shift has taken place in the Millennial and Gen Z sets. It is alarming to see a downward spiral of the theological framework in young people. All of the studies are proving this, none clearer than the 2018 Barna Group findings showing Gen Z with a 4 percent biblical worldview. This loss of theology has had a lot to do with the rise of the sexual revolution in America.

As I stated in my last book, *ythology: The Study of Youth*, when the church and the family lost their theological ethic, we lost our young people.

Each of these changes have created a revolution in their own era, from the 1920s up until today. There is a redefining wave of sexuality crashing over our society.

But it seems with every revolution has come a free run away from the Bible and a worsening of values. We have watched the government take a step back by redefining marriage, the media take a step back by censoring little, our schools creating progressive sex education in the classroom, parents removed from the equation when it comes to their kids getting abortions, and society's broadening of gender identity definitions. Through all of this, our own twenty-first century sexual revolution has put all of the other revolutions in America to shame.

There are many reasons for the rise of the present sexual revolution in America. It is influenced over time by progressive education, a loss of conservative censorship in the media, an entertainment industry pushing the envelope with humanistic and postmodern thought breakaway from conservatism, the dramatic loss of theology in Gen Z...and, on top of everything else, the silence of the church. Each of these influences have contributed to the social and sexuality changes we are seeing in our nation right now.

> But, undeniably, one of the main reasons why we see such an overwhelming and comprehensive counterculture of sexuality rising in America is because of the communication age that we are living in.

Sex and porn are so much more accessible to this generation. [As pastors and parents, we] need to become vigilant in stressing the importance of social media and purity.
—Dylan McKneely, youth pastor

It is so much faster and easier to bring about change because information does not have to travel through relational networks in person or a telephone call between friends. Today, information travels immediately through conference calls, convention meetings, radio and television broadcasts, and innumerable social platforms and apps that are instantly accessible globally in the palm of our hand. This information age has created a breakaway from the classic and conservative avenue and onto the modern and progressive mainstream freeway.

Earlier, I shared a quote from Hugh Hefner that illustrates the kind of mainstream breakaway we see today in America. As Hefner noted, once-held moral beliefs have been sacrificed, leading to "a lot of hurt and hypocrisy"—and, I will add, materialism, idolatry, and deception. Our human effort to change what were once deeply held truths into a shallow framework of personal relativism has happened because we have either left, or have not known, a true theology of God. Hefner wanted "to change things in some positive way so that people could choose...alternate personal ways of living their lives."

And change things he did.

I'm sure if you could have shown a photo of this present sexual revolution to your grandparents fifty years ago, they would have thought a three-ring circus came to town. In a world that is polytheistic and polysexual, believing in a spectrum of gods and sexuality, we could use some standardization or truth in the world. To jump off this modern and progressive mainstream freeway and back on to the classic and conservative avenue.

At the beginning of a book like this, standardization could turn most of the Western mind off. What do I mean by that? The Western mind is a mix of postmodern, humanistic, and Christian thought. A system that builds morality from the broad spectrum of *relativism for the postmodern*, *natural law for the humanist*, without supernatural laws or God's sovereign involvement, and *biblical non-negotiables of Christians*. What a mix.

The twenty-first century is a *poly* century, with multiple belief systems. There is no room for standardization or common sense biblical absolutes, especially when it comes to sexuality and religion. The Western mind has no room for that kind of closed spiritual code or belief. Yet, remember from the preface, all of us have a set of standards—i.e., standardization—that we work from. It's called our framework or box.

As it relates to the sexual revolution, some will read my box and turn me off because I have a certain lens through which I'm writing this book and commentating on the Scriptures. Even with my commitment to be as unbiased as possible, I understand I have an upbringing and a framework. So, if you are turning me off, maybe you should understand that *you* too have an upbringing or framework that shapes *your* thinking. For most of the young people reading this, the box will help because they have never journeyed through this information.

Looking at the definitions of sexuality brings us to where we are today. Our generation is living in what may be the most dramatic sexual revolution America has ever seen. Let me define what I see in society right now.

This current sexual revolution can be defined as the redefinition or the breakaway of once common sexuality beliefs from the previous generation—a breakaway from beliefs such as defining *gender identity* as male or female, *marriage* as between a man and woman, *illicit and immoral sexual relationships* outside of marriage as sin, and *censorship* of specific norms or codes of language and behavior in media as a necessary good.

> *The present redefinition and breakaway now looks like gender identity **additions** such as LGBTQ+, **open** marriage between genders, **illicit** and immoral sexual relationships becoming normative, **uncensored** media expression, and many more shifts we will talk about throughout this book.*

The Mills and Gen Z are growing up in the aftermath of a lot of problems that have swept through their culture.

Present cultural issues such as the broken family, an age of terror and war, a divided government, a media and entertainment industry that has lost censorship, school and campus violence, the opioid crisis, rising university costs, racial tensions, the overwhelming imbalance of social media platforms, and the COVID-19 pandemic have all left their mark on this generation. Although I believe the greatest problem for young people today is the broken family (something we will detail later in this book), each of these problems, in their own way, cause young people an ominous wave of emotion every day the sun rises and sets.

But, arguably, there is one issue looming over all of these others.

We used to consider a societal generation as roughly eighty years. The rapid technological changes that occurred during the twentieth century led to the advent of the forty-year model as a lifespan for human development. Today, some sociologists create social models in research that see a generation shift taking place about every decade or so. This is part of the reason why so much change is happening so quickly. I don't know about you, but that change is exhausting and difficult to keep up with.

THE TIMES THEY ARE A-CHANGIN'

The words are iconic. Written more than fifty years ago, Bob Dylan penned the words so prophetic they could be sung today:

Come mothers and fathers

Throughout the land

And don't criticize

What you can't understand

Your sons and your daughters

Are beyond your command

Your old road is rapidly agin'

Please get out of the new one

If you can't lend your hand

For the times they are a-changin'[4]

So what is changing today? What does the sexual revolution actually look like? Here is an introduction to a few things that will be addressed more fully in the coming chapters.

MARRIAGE

Marriage doesn't seem as sacred anymore. The statistics are basically unchanging...but just under half of all marriages end in divorce. According to the United Nations, America has the third highest divorce rate in the world. The causes of divorce include marrying too young, infidelity, abuse, and financial strain.[5]

In addition to failing marriages, the time-honored universally accepted marriage is no longer sacred between a man and a woman. What has been socially acceptable from the beginning of time and almost without exception is now shifting right before our eyes. We're now using language such as union, civil agreement, and partnership. Although marriage definitions are changing and happening at a mind-blowing pace, this isn't an entirely new direction.

Gay marriage in medieval Europe can be dated back to the thirteenth century, when male-bonding ceremonies were common in churches

---

4. Bob Dylan, title track on *The Times They Are A-Changin'* (Columbia Records, 1964).
5. United Nations Statistics Division, "Marriage and divorce" (https://unstats.un.org/unsd/demographic-social/sconcerns/mar_divorce).

across the Mediterranean. Apart from the couples' gender, these rare events were almost indistinguishable from other marriages of the era. Look at this description of marriage in the 1300s:

> Twelfth-century liturgies for same-sex unions—also known as "spiritual brotherhoods"—included the recital of marriage prayers, the joining of hands at the altar, and a ceremonial kiss. Some historians believe these unions were merely a way to seal alliances and business deals. But Eric Berkowitz, author of *Sex and Punishment*, says it is "difficult to believe that these rituals did not contemplate erotic contact. In fact, it was the sex between the men involved that later caused same-sex unions to be banned." That happened in 1306, when the Byzantine Emperor Andronicus II declared such ceremonies, along with sorcery and incest, to be unchristian.[6]

We will look into this more fully in a later chapter.

GENDER

Another proof of the impact of the sexual revolution is the gender arena.

The first known gender reassignment surgery took place in 1930, but such procedures were rare until 1966, when Johns Hopkins University Medical Center began to provide them.

> The idea of gender has become more of a personal preference, rather than a genetic creation state. The goal with a student who is struggling with their gender identity is not to detach them from their feelings. Rather it's channeling their feelings into a place that is better for their spiritual well-being.
> —Dylan McKneely, youth pastor

---

6. Claudia Rapp, *Brotherhood-Making in Late Antiquity and Byzantium: Monks, Laymen, and Christian Ritual* (New York, NY: Oxford University Press, 2016).

The definition and the framework of gender throughout history has mostly been binary—that is, male or female. Binary is a mathematical concept that uses only two numbers: one and zero. Computers operate in binary: true or false, on or off, yes or no. The binary argument or definition of gender comes from the biblical account in Genesis of the creation of humankind, which we'll look at in the next chapter on theology.

However, this *binary* acceptance of gender is changing quickly and becoming a *nonbinary* discussion. The *nonbinary* argument or definition allows for multiple equations for gender identity. This can be seen in the assorted gender terms that have been created, the social discussion becoming more progressive, and the added box titled "other" on informational forms.

In the last three years, Canada became a world leader in gender-neutral greetings, airline protocol, nonbinary birth certificates, and even legislation to rewrite the Canadian national anthem to include "all of us" rather than "thy sons." However, what may be even more unique in Canada, and globally, is something else.

> *A Canadian baby born in 2017 has the first non-gender designation on their health card. The parent, a nonbinary transgender person, says, "It is up to [the baby] to decide how they identify, when they are old enough to develop their own gender identity."*[7]

Systematically, globally, a shift is taking place in all arenas of the sexual revolution.

For instance, in the lead-up to the presidential election of 2020, Democratic nominee Joe Biden was asked in a town hall on October 15 about the freedoms for children who want to have a sex change. He

---

7. Zamira Rahim, "Canadian baby given health card without sex designation," CNN, July 5, 2017 (www.cnn.com/2017/07/04/health/canadian-baby-gender-designation/index.html).

replied, "The idea that an eight-year-old child or a ten-year-old child decides 'I want to be transgender, that's what I think I'd like to be, it would make my life a lot easier.' There should be no discrimination...." I still cannot believe this is where we are in our world today. It is more proof of the degeneration and the loss of morality in our culture.

Now, I'm not agreeing that we should discriminate—against anyone.

But is that how we are going to handle our children? Just let them, in their adolescence, decide their life will be easier if they get a gender change? That they can have hormones on demand and get a sex change to fix their problems? Children—and adults for that matter—change their minds *in the drive-through* about whether to get large or small fries, a hamburger or a salad. And we want to let a child make a gender change decision?

To allow a child to determine their sex is ignorant and reckless adult behavior. And furthermore, to allow them to *think* that their life fulfillment is determined by their gender is ludicrous. What we are saying with this kind of rhetoric is senseless. I know *adults* who fantasize about body image surgeries and then change their minds. How is allowing an underdeveloped child to make that life-altering decision a sensible thing to do?

Wouldn't it be better to sit down and speak to the child and help them through the confusion or bullying they might be getting rather than affirming adolescent desires and ultimately allowing a sex change to change their life outcomes? Wouldn't we rather teach our children coping skills and emotional strength rather than solving their problems with a gender change?

What makes this even more unbelievable is that we have descended into calling anyone who would challenge nonbinary behavior a bigot because they are judgmental and intolerant. The shift is happening right before our eyes. And it won't stop at transgender operations.

Let's look at the next proof of the impact of the sexual revolution on our culture.

HOMOSEXUALITY

The sexual revolution taking place in America over the last twenty-five years has dramatically changed the course of homosexuality. The evidence for this is abounding, but no doubt it had its momentum in the gay movement coining the phrase "coming out of the closet" or simply "coming out." A quick look at the history of this concept is telling.

> *It actually began as emancipation in Germany in the mid-1800s. A much more progressive society than the U.S. at the time, Germany's gay emancipation still did not catch on and was basically held underground or behind closed doors.*

It wasn't until the early 1940s in America that a movement of homosexuals became more vocal. However, that movement would wait another forty years before what most consider the real "coming out" moment would be. In October 1987, the first National Coming Out day took place in Washington and resulted in the organization of many of the gay movements still existing today.

Does culture, tradition, and society really have that much power over an individual? Why would centuries of belief and tradition now change so drastically in the last twenty-five years? How can an individual in society move so quickly through discovery of being homosexual, coming to terms with it, gaining a following, and now support organizations and services? I believe part of the answer is the power of the communications age being able to stay consistently on top of the narrative.

But there was another influence that added to the "coming out." An undeniable shift in how homosexuality is viewed in culture came about from the acceptance of religious voices in the discussion and the growth of homosexuality in the American church.

This may have never been more true than when Pope Francis made this revolutionary statement in an interview a few years ago:

> A person once asked me, in a provocative manner, if I approved of homosexuality. I replied with another question: "Tell me: when God looks at a gay person, does he endorse the existence of this person with love, or reject and condemn this person?" We must always consider the person. Here we enter into the mystery of the human being. In life, God accompanies persons, and we must accompany them, starting from their situation. It is necessary to accompany them with mercy. When that happens, the Holy Spirit inspires the priest to say the right thing. This is also the great benefit of confession as a sacrament: evaluating case by case and discerning what is the best thing to do for a person who seeks God and grace. The confessional is not a torture chamber, but the place in which the Lord's mercy motivates us to do better.[8]

"The confessional is not a torture chamber." That really hit me hard.

In the beginning of the interview, Pope Francis said, "I am a sinner." This would be quite prophetic since he was later asked about homosexuality. While some people were looking for a stricter condemnation from Pope Francis, they may have missed this for whatever reason. It was there. What became front and center was how Pope Francis certainly opened eyes globally by placing the emphasis of his thoughts on our pastoral approach to people and not just their sin. The pope's view on homosexuality requiring repentance is very clear if you consider the whole interview and the totality of his statements. But what cannot be lost is his emphasis on treating people with mercy.

In a 2019 interview, the pope emphasized that families should not shun their homosexual relatives, saying:

---

8. Antonio Spadaro, "A Big Heart Open to God: An interview with Pope Francis," *America: The Jesuit Review of Faith & Culture,* September 30, 2013 (www.americamagazine.org/faith/2013/09/30/big-heart-open-god-interview-pope-francis).

People with homosexual orientation have a right to be in the family and parents have the right to recognize that son as homosexual, that daughter as homosexual. Nobody should be thrown out of the family, or be made miserable because of it.[9]

Pope Francis also indicated that he believes homosexuals should be able to join together through a civil union rather than marriage.[10]

LGBTQ+

It is difficult to even separate sexual *identity* or *behaviors* or *dispositions* into a small category anymore. Our culture has definitely added to the nonbinary sex status in the past few years. I have recently researched more than forty-five different terms and definitions for sex gender, sex identity, sex dispositions, and sex identifications. This investigation has been exhausting and telling of the breakaway from the classical and traditional theology of sexuality.

Here are just a few of these—because it would most likely take about two or three pages to list them all:

- *Binary*: restricting gender to two types or categories, male and female

- *Nonbinary*: allowing for more than two gender types or categories (LGBTQ+)

- *Heterosexual*: the attraction to a gender different from one's own

- *Homosexual*: the attraction to a gender the same as one's own (gay)

9. "Pope Francis' homosexuality comments heavily edited in documentary, Vatican has no comment on civil unions," Catholic News Agency, October 20, 2020 (www.catholicnewsagency.com/news/pope-francis-homosexuality-comments-heavily-edited-in-documentary-no-vatican-comment-on-civil-union-88210).
10. Ibid.

- *Lesbian*: women who are attracted only to other women
- *Bisexual*: attracted to two or more genders
- *Pansexual*: attracted to all genders or unconcerned with gender
- *Bicurious*: open to experiment with multiple genders
- *Polysexual*: attracted to many genders
- *Monosexual*: attracted to only one gender
- *Androsexual*: attracted to masculine gender presentation
- *Gynosexual*: attracted to feminine gender presentation
- *Questioning*: people debating their own sexuality/gender
- *Asexual*: not experiencing sexual attraction; the term *ace* is also used
- *Demisexual*: one who only experiences sexual attraction after forming a strong emotional bond
- *Perioriented*: when sexual and romantic orientation targets the same gender set
- *Varioriented*: when sexual and romantic orientations do not target the same gender set
- *Erasure*: ignoring the existence of genders and sexualities in the middle of the spectrum
- *Polyamorous*: people having sex with multiple people simultaneously
- *AFAB*: assigned female at birth
- *AMAB*: assigned male at birth

To see the impact of the most recent sexual revolution on the LGBTQ+ community, one need only look at the "+" in gender and dispositional lists. The *evolution* of the plus (+) on LGBTQ—an acronym for lesbian, gay, bisexual, transgender, and questioning (or sometimes queer)—is a testament of the *revolution* of this growth in the sex gender nonconforming (GNC) arena.

Here is the last revolution happening today.

SEXUAL IMMORALITY

This concept will be exhausted in this book because when talking about sexual immorality, we are talking about a broad topic. Even the root language can change. Specifically, sexual immorality can be defined personally depending on your moral framework. In this book, we will baseline our definition of sexual immorality from the Bible as *unnatural promiscuous sexual practices.*

> *The following sexual practices will be included as sexual immorality: gender nonbinary behavior (as opposed to feelings), adultery, sex before marriage, pornography, incest, bestiality, homosexuality, cyber-sex, sexting, prostitution or human trafficking, and self-sex.*

The Mayo Clinic lists several reasons for compulsive sexual promiscuity: family conflict, addictions, physical or sexual abuse, mental health conditions, and relationship problems. The clinic defines promiscuity as "a compulsive sexual behavior outside of social ideals and norms." It's an interesting medical description of this term—and it's similar to how we will find Paul describing this concept from two passages of Scripture. I'm going to deal with each of these later, so I'm merely mentioning them here.

GENERATIONAL LOSS

Why is a society so susceptible to these sweeping reforms in sexuality in a matter of a quarter of a century? I have to admit, I'm not sure, but I will try to detail several reasons why throughout this book. Maybe part of the answer can be found in the technological term *generational loss.*

The idea behind *generational loss* is a good way to see the sexual revolution taking place in America.

Generational loss is what happens with analog tapes and audio that is transferred through multiple processes.[11] Every copy of an original tape and audio source is known as a generation, or a transfer, and each subsequent copy of this source will become degraded to some extent in the transfer process.

A sexual revolution has the same effect upon our original source material. There is a loss in every generation as we get further and further from it. The breakaway we are seeing now is definitive.

Many will not build their worldview on the same source. Some will build their worldview on personal feelings, some on pop cultural norms, and others on subjective moral reasoning.

What I am defining as the original source here is the Bible.

I believe greater clarity on a topic or issue comes when we start with what the Bible clearly defines or commands about a subject. When we lose sight of that original source, we have generational loss.

For example, when the Bible states that God created male and female, and all of history has supported this, the main reason we have had such a sweeping change in the last twenty-five years is because we have had generational biblical loss. Such loss has been caused by things like *progressive education,* a *loss of conservative censorship* in the media, an *entertainment industry pushing the envelope* of conservative action, and systematic *humanistic and postmodern* breakaway from the Scriptures.

---

11. "Generational Loss," Sweetwater Sound, September 5, 2000 (www.sweetwater. com/insync/generational-loss).

> *The generational loss that has caused the free run of
> the sexual revolution in America is in large part the
> responsibility of the church losing its voice in homes and in
> culture. Because silence is the enemy of truth.*

FINALLY

If we lose God, we lose love. If we lose love, we lose sexuality.

Before his passing in April 2020, Sy Rogers struggled with a trans- and homosexual lifestyle until his conversion to Christ in 1978. Sy had a big impact upon my life. We had spoken personally many times and even had the privilege of speaking alongside of each other in conference settings. His wife called me after his death and thanked me for our friendship.

Sy was a healing voice in the relationship between the church and the gay community. Whether speaking or writing, Sy often said, "Redemption for me wasn't getting married. It was finding the love of Christ." This statement captures the emptiness of a loveless sexuality.

I am not saying that someone cannot love if they are sexually dysfunctional. What I am saying is that Christ's love is sufficient aside from any other love. So really, a loveless sexuality is idolatry because it places upon another what is reserved only for God. I truly believe that sexual sin is idolatry because it is placing a greater love upon ourselves or another person than our purest love and affection for Christ.

We cannot lose God at the center of our society. Because if we lose God, we lose love. And if we lose love, we lose the discussion. And if we lose the discussion, we lose a generation. The church's greatest responsibility is to preach the good news of Christ to our society. When the church fails to do that, *social* movements lead the way, not *spiritual* movements. What we desperately need today is another spiritual revolution to come up fiercely beside the current sexual revolution with truth and love!

Many of the arguments in the human sexuality arena tend to begin from a subjective moral reasoning in culture, from ideology, from statistics, from the populace (prevalence), history, biology, or even legislation in government and law. However, I do not believe we begin a moral argument from these kinds of things. Rather, the moral argument should not begin with subjective moral reasoning in *culture*— or in personal ideology or statistics or populace and prevalence or history or biology or the government and law. Each of these things must submit to the objective moral argument in the *Scriptures*.

Why?

> *Let me share a great part of the reason why we must be careful to base our discussions upon truth. Dr. John Corvino, a gay author and debater, wrote in his book, Debating Same-Sex Marriage, "Both sides of the debate bring forth extensive statistics and expert research testimony leaving the average observer confused."*

Think about that. We cannot derive our box or truth structure from something that is confusing and changing. We must derive our truth structure from something that is clear and unchanging. The purity of the argument is not extra-biblical. It is presented in the Bible. And we must always return to the elite exegetical and hermeneutic principles of studying the Bible.

The degeneration of values in a revolution can be seen in ever-increasing spiritual change. Where there is a loss of the original biblical relationship, there is a breakaway that is undeniable. The dilemma is not solely about *social movements* in culture leading the way in a sexual revolution. The dilemma is more about *spiritual movements* in the church losing their way in the sexual revolution.

My prayer for the sexual revolution moment we are in right now is that our faith will be tested—and shown to be real. My prayer is that we will raise a generation of teenagers who understand the complete theology of God so the testing of their faith will result in their faith being spread.

A counterrevolution will need to take place, a *revival* happening in the church that brings about an *awakening* in culture. The truest sense of revivals do not take place necessarily in culture. The *revival* takes place in the church coming back to its life purpose. It is an *awakening* that takes place in culture when the lost are brought to life in the church.

> Why is this true? Because often revolutions (in the bad sense) happen in **rebellion**—rebellion to God and His ideas. But often, too, revolutions (in the good sense) happen in **obedience** to God and His ideas.

A LOVE REVOLUTION

Ultimately, we need to counter the sexual revolution in our *culture* with a love revolution in the *church*! We cannot continue to move in the direction we are moving because the direction we are moving is away from a relationship to culture. Remember, if the devil steals love, he steals sexuality. So we, as the church, must fight then for a loving sexuality ethic in Scripture, or we will continue to create a loveless sexuality ethic in our culture that separates the church from it altogether.

It is not enough to rage against the lie. You've got to replace it with the truth. —Bono, U2

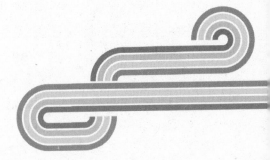

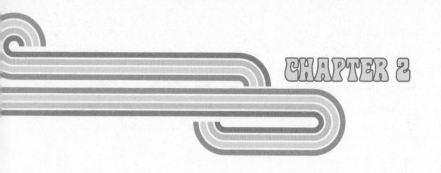

CHAPTER 2

A THEOLOGY OF SEXUALITY

God Is Love

In the movie *Catch Me If You Can*,[12] Frank Abagnale (portrayed by
Leonardo DiCaprio) is notorious for being fraudulently employed as
a doctor, a lawyer, and a co-pilot, all before reaching his twenty-first
birthday. As a successful con artist, Abagnale also becomes adept at
check fraud and steals millions of dollars. FBI Agent Carl Hanratty
(Tom Hanks) makes it his responsibility to capture Abagnale and bring
him to justice. However, Abagnale remains one step ahead of Hanratty
and the federal agents.

Abagnale is eventually caught and imprisoned, but Hanratty convinces
the FBI to let Abagnale serve the rest of his sentence working for the
FBI bank fraud unit. In a riveting scene, Abagnale tells the federal
agents that you don't learn to spot counterfeit checks by studying the
counterfeits. Instead, you study genuine checks until you have mastered
the look of the real thing.

> As we take a look at the theology of sexuality, I fear we have
> been looking at **counterfeit cultural sexuality** for so long
> that we do not recognize **genuine scriptural sexuality**.

---

12. *Catch Me If You Can*, directed by Steven Spielberg (2002; DreamWorks Pictures).

We must look more intently at Scripture than culture, or we will never be able to see the genuine. A thorough understanding of Scripture stands against the counterfeit of culture and a thorough understanding of theology against the counterfeit of our society.

GOD IS LOVE

Love. Agape. Eros. Philia. Storgé. Amor. Ai. Hubun. Grá. Sneha. Anpu. Liebe. Liubov. Yêu. Rak. A look at love around the world. Love is the greatest. Love is eternal. Love is unfathomable.

That is why love is the best word to begin with for a book on sexuality. Because sexuality is not complete without love. And since God is love, sexuality cannot be complete without a theological understanding of God.

The Bible says that God is *love*. In 1 John 4:8, John is quoted directly as saying, "*God is love.*" What is so interesting about this text is that John also stresses to each of us that we are known as believers by our love. Love is the inescapable quality of Christianity!

A discussion on sexuality today cannot be done without a basic understanding of the highest form of love: agape. Meaning unconditional charity, the deepest Christian fellowship and communion created by God and shared with humankind.

God's character and nature is no secret in the Scriptures. There are many verses in the Bible that define the character and the nature of God directly and indirectly. For instance, God is also called *all-knowing, all-powerful, all-present, good, merciful, compassionate, just, terrible, awesome, fearful, patient, perfect, gracious,* and *merciful.* However, the foundational and elementary nature of God is love. That means we understand everything about God through His love.

> *No matter how we acquired our views on sexuality—*
> *whether a **personal** sexuality ethic or a **social** sexuality*
> *ethic—I contend sexuality can only be understood through*
> *having a **scriptural or biblical** understanding of God.*

Because sexuality began in the image of God as Creator, our understanding of sexuality then must be anchored to the fact that **God is love**. This must be the *modus operandi* (method of operation, or M.O.) or worldview or framework by which we understand God.

God cannot operate outside of His character. Everything He does can be defined by His M.O. That infers when God created us at the beginning of time back in Genesis 1–3, we can only be fully known through His love.

In the same way, all of us have an M.O., worldview, or framework by which we see the world. The reality is that not every person's M.O. is an *objective* moral reasoning built out of the *Scriptures*. It is more popular to build a *subjective* moral reasoning out of personal ideology or *culture*.

If we have a biblical worldview, our method of operation will be love. It really cannot be anything else—not selfish, not cultural, not judgmental, and not hateful. To understand the Scriptures is to understand God. And to understand God is to understand love.

GOD IS HOLY

About the time we come to understand that God is love, multiple writers, including Moses, David, the prophets, and Peter, called God *holy*. Wow, what a mix of character. To see God as *love* and *holy* at the same time is remarkable. What a responsibility Christians have to model to this world a God of both *love* and *holiness*. It is almost too difficult of a task without His *grace* and His *truth*.

Do you see the connection? We see that God is *love* by His *grace,* and yet we see God as *holy* by His *truth*. I believe the entire list of God's character and His nature given to us by all of the authors in Scripture falls between His *love* and *holiness*, or His *grace* and *truth*.

> I'm a virgin because I follow what the Bible says about sex. It talks in Genesis about how when a man and woman make love, they become one flesh. I think it's cool to say "they make love" and not "they make sex."
>
> —Jack, age 17

A SEXUALITY BOX

As I pointed out in the first chapter, we cannot lose another generation to theological ignorance. If we are going to contribute to the reforming of sexuality to a scriptural set, theology, and not culture, must be at the center of our lives. Parents, teenagers, and youth leaders must develop a *genuine scriptural sexuality* or we will never be able to recognize the *counterfeit cultural sexuality* going on right before our eyes.

Dare we call the cultural wave that has crashed on the shore of American youth culture and wreaked havoc on a generation of young people *the Abagnale Effect*? We have looked so long at the counterfeit that we do not recognize the original.

4 PERCENT WORLDVIEW

Again, the box is our framework or worldview or ethic or theology. Our box is the place where our principles are created. Let's admit it from the beginning: all of us have a certain box we live in. Our box of information, relationships, and experiences is what shapes our worldview and the framework for our thinking, attitudes, and, ultimately, our actions. But when it comes to morality, everyone should be operating within the same box. A universal set of ethics.

Let me explain by looking at Gen Z, the teenagers today who were born around 1998.

I know it has been popular for many years for people to get out of a box and escape routines. It has been popular for some to say, "I think outside the box." It's like a badge of courage. However, when it comes to an emerging generation called Gen Z, breaking out of the box has been devastating to their theology.

> According to a study by the Barna Group and the Impact 360 Institute, only 4 percent of Gen Z has a biblical worldview.[13] Wow. Just think about this. I didn't believe it when I heard it. This means that 4 percent of teens in America **think** Christian. With Christian doctrine in mind. And as a lens by which they see everything else in life. The vast majority **don't** think that way.

A biblical worldview, in a very real sense, is when people live out their most fundamental beliefs in everyday life according to the Bible. When we have a biblical worldview, the Bible affects the way we think and everything we do.

Can you see how important the theology of a generation is now? What have we done—or not done—to take our young people to these lowly depths of theological formation? I think this statistic is the reason why we are staring at the loss of sexuality absolutes today in a generation.

---

13. Jonathan Morrow, "Only 4 Percent of Gen Z Have a Biblical Worldview," Impact 360 Institute (www.impact360institute.org/articles/4-percent-gen-z-biblical-worldview).

> *Because our students do not think theologically, they are formulating their sexuality ethic from a **counterfeit** cultural view, instead of an **authentic scriptural** view.*

Furthermore, Gen Z Christians can only name half of the Ten Commandments. This lack of a biblical moral reference is shaping a whole new generation's thought on everything, and not just sexuality.

As we will see in the social sexuality chapter, Gen Z is actually quite comfortable in a box. They really do not mind an understood structure or way of doing things, unlike their older brothers and sisters, the Millennials. So operating out of a box or set of rules or standards is okay. It brings them comfort, and they are then able to work the box and challenge it a bit. Grace is important to the Gen Z set, their relationships within a box and an understanding of how loyal their squad will be to them no matter their beliefs or circumstances.

> *Given this research, I contend what we really need is a box. A code or ceiling, walls or a fence. A lens by which we see everything. Because otherwise, we land where we are today, with everyone's subjective personal ideology or version of truth on all kind of matters.*

To me, the box, or code, or ceiling, or walls, or fences are the Scriptures in the Bible. Maybe that is not true for you. Either way, I just happen to believe we are all created by God and expected to live by His standards. That deep down inside all of us—every one of us, whether we admit it or not—there is a hole in our soul only God can fill. The government, education, the corporate world, entertainment, social media, relationships, status, sex, or materialism cannot fill that hole. It is the inerrant and infallible truth in the Bible that is going to fill the hole in humanity.

Sure, we may read the same biblical text and arrive at different views. But hopefully, we are going to see there are some universal absolutes in Scripture as it relates to sexuality that we can all gather around. The important part of this project to me is really simple: getting to the answer to the problem of sexuality by Scripture and not by culture. Getting to the answer from an absolute box and not a changing one.

MY PERSONAL ETHIC SOUNDBITE

Building a box to start with really is hard to put in an accurate soundbite in an information age so great at taking our words out of context and nailing us to the public wall. I'm going to risk it anyway and give you my personal soundbite on the topic of sexuality. Hopefully, the clarity for my personal ethic will come throughout the book, however, if you have to pin me to a soundbite, read the following.

> *The sexual revolution going on in America today with regard to **sexual identity issues**, **the sanctity of marriage**, and **sexual promiscuity** is part of a sexual disorder contrary to clearly stated biblical principles. Principles found in the words of Moses in the book of Genesis, Solomon in Proverbs, Jesus in Matthew, Paul in Romans and other texts, Jude in the book of Jude, and John in Revelation. Principles defining the creation of humankind as male and female, the sanctity of marriage between a man and a woman, and the sanctity of romantic and sexual relationships between a man and woman within marriage.*

As I mentioned in the preface, almost everyone who has ever written on this topic promises to look at the Scriptures in an unbiased way, from both sides of the argument. The hard part is making sure a person's M.O. or their *objective* moral reasoning is based out of the Scriptures and not a *subjective* moral reasoning based out of personal ideology or culture.

A THEOLOGY OF SEXUALITY

As we begin, let's form a framework for the theology and worldview of sexuality from a biblical perspective. There are several places to acquire a scriptural sexuality ethic, including, but not limited to, Genesis 1–3, 19; Proverbs 5–10; Matthew 5, 15, and 19; Romans 1; Galatians 5; 1 Corinthians 6–7; Jude 5–8; and Revelation 2, 18, 21, and 22. Each of these texts clearly add to the discussion on sexuality, but there are so many other similar texts that I will allude to in reference to these.

Before we do some commentary, let me begin with language. It will help to understand some of the concepts in their original or root meanings. When we look at the root meanings of words, it is much easier to determine what the text says. This is one of the principles of *exegesis*. When we look at the context or setting of these words, it is one of the principles of *hermeneutics*. I am taking the glossary of definitions from the *Abingdon Strong's Greek Concordance and Lexicon* because it is the most widely accepted tool used in good exegesis and hermeneutic study.

HEBREW WORDS IN THE SEXUALITY DISCUSSION

- yada: *"To know deeply, learn, perceive"*

- erva: *"Sex; uncover nakedness; know in a sexual context"*

- shekobeth, shakab: *"Copulation, lying down to have sex"*

- ishshah: *"Woman, wife, female"*

- math: *"Male, man"*

- zanah: *"To commit fornication, sex outside of covenantal marriage, harlotry"*

- kerithuth: *"Divorcement or to put away"*

GREEK WORDS IN THE SEXUALITY DISCUSSION

- porneia: *"Fornication, illicit sexual relations outside of marriage, to sell off purity, idolatry"*

- heteros: *"Another, other, not same nature"*

- sarkos: *"Strange flesh, body, human nature"*

- arsenokoitai: *"Male intercourse on beds together"*

- malakos: *"Uncertain affinity, metaphorically in a bad sense, soft, flexible, delicate"*

ADDITIONAL WORDS

Here are some word/concept explanations that will be mentioned for doing accurate biblical study from other word study tools:

- exegesis: *"The critical explanation of a biblical text to discover its originally intended meaning."*

- hermeneutics: *"The complete study and integrity of the principles and methods used to interpret the biblical text."*

- midrash: *"The exposition or interpretation of Old Testament writings"*

It is important to understand the basics of the language and the words used in the biblical texts we will look at throughout this book.

Sometimes I feel like I don't know what I believe.
—Jesse, age 13

SEVEN ETHICS ON SEXUALITY

With those definitions out of the way, let me give you the ethics that shape my thinking on sexuality as we study the Scriptures and try to determine accurate exegesis and hermeneutic commentary. These are my seven ethics on building a theology of sexuality. See if they help you to shape your worldview on sexuality as you read through these.

1. THEOLOGICAL FRAMEWORK

Our personal sexuality belief will come from culture or from Scripture. It is our ideological (or cultural) and theological (or scriptural) framework. It will be changing if it comes from culture, but constant if it comes from Scripture. That is why the arguments have changed in the cultural arena and yet have stayed the same in the scriptural arena. It is important that we see how history treated sexuality in both Scripture and culture, in both conservative and progressive ways. However, we must be careful to emphasize culture or history over Scripture. Why? Because a scriptural ethic is a static moral framework that does not shift with trends or time.

2. CAREFUL HERMENEUTICS AND EXEGESIS

We look at and interpret Scripture differently. It is common to read theologians on all sides of the sexuality argument who disagree with each other. That is why it is vital—foundational—for us to conduct an unbiased hermeneutical and exegetical study of the Bible.

Here is one quote from Robin Scroggs, a well-known author/ theologian who was a moderate on the issue of sexual immorality and homosexuality. Summing up many of the statements in commentaries I have read through the years, and speaking of Romans 1, Scroggs said:

> It cannot fairly be said that Paul is incensed against homo-sexuality. That he opposes it, on the other hand, is not to be denied.

What a general statement appealing to both sides of the argument and carefully positioning all sides on this issue.

3. CONSTRUCTS IN HUMAN SEXUALITY THEOLOGY

Look at Genesis 1–3, 19; Leviticus 18, 20; Proverbs 5–9; Matthew 5, 15, 19; Romans 1; 1 Corinthians 6–7; Jude 5–8; and Revelation 3, 18, 21, and 22. In these texts, Moses, Solomon, Jesus, Paul, Jude, and John did have something to say about the *sacredness of human sexuality* as male and female; the *sacredness of human sexuality and marriage* between a man and a woman; and the *sacredness of human sexuality and sex* between a man and a woman within marriage. Differences aside, there are enough clear guidelines in Scripture to agree on.

4. THESE TEXTS TEACH US THREE MAIN SUPPOSITIONS

First, what we do know conclusively from these texts is that *God created two genders in the human species—male and female.* Second, *God kept the sanctity of marriage between a man and a woman.* And third, *God defined natural sexual relations between a man and a woman within the marriage union.* Any deviation from that nature, form, or ethic was not the intent of Scripture and becomes a secondary unnatural order, a cultural or personal order and not a scriptural order that has shifted over time.

5. OTHER VERSES ON THE SUBJECT

There are many other verses inspired by the Holy Spirit to other authors who spoke on this subject. But they are too numerous to cover in this setting. These texts include many of the same words and phrases used in those listed above. They give definitions or prohibitions on our three topics of gender, marriage, and sexual immorality (binary, nonbinary, adultery, fornication, prostitution, idolatry, abnormality, incest, bestiality, and homosexuality). These texts are Leviticus 18; Deuteronomy 22; Judges 19; Psalm 38; Proverbs 30; Song of Solomon; Jeremiah 13; Acts 15; Romans 13; and 2 Peter 2. I have learned that a holistic reading of the entire Bible is clear about gender, marriage, and sexual immorality.

6. LOOK AT THE BIG PICTURE

Look at the macro or explicit picture of sexuality in the Bible, as much as the micro or implicit picture. Sometimes people get fixated on one or two texts when it comes to sexuality, sex, sexual immorality, or sexual promiscuity. It can be easy to spend time on a few of the key texts and to take them apart with our own personal lens. But the whole of Scripture—including the *Torah, legal and civil codes, Psalms, the book of Wisdom, poetry, the prophets, the Gospels, the Epistles, and the apocalyptic Revelation*—each of these always address healthy sexuality ethics with the precept of a man and a woman in marriage. Of course, there are unhealthy sexuality statements between a man and a woman in the Bible also. But those references are simply reality, lessons to be learned, and certainly not endorsed examples or patterns of God's design.

7. EXEGETICAL DIFFERENCES SHOULD NOT DIVIDE US

So we may have a different interpretation of sexuality in the Scriptures than others do. Maybe you believe, as I have stated in this book, that *gender* identity is binary, that *marriage* is between a man and a woman, and that *sex* before marriage, outside of marriage, or with the same sex is unnatural. Or maybe you do not believe the way of this book. Whatever our differences, just because someone believes differently than we do, what right does that give us to treat them with partiality or judgment?

One of the greatest lessons I want you to learn in this book is never to win an argument and lose a relationship. Hopefully, these ethics will help guide you to a truthful and loving framework for your personal sexuality belief.

THEOLOGICAL COMMENTARY

> In Genesis 1, God emphatically declares His creation to be good. In Genesis 2, something was no longer good. The solution God employed was a coming together of male and female, in unity and yet sexually diverse, to fully express the heart of the One every human—regardless of ethnicity, socioeconomic background, religious upbringing, or gender—craves.
> —Heath Adamson, global director, Next Generation Commission

With that in mind, let's do a simple exegetical and hermeneutical review of our main texts.

GENESIS 1–3, 5

The first principle of sexuality in the Bible is found in Genesis 1–3 and 5.

This text is called *the Genesis intent*, or the creation intent of sexuality. This is Moses's account of the beginning of humankind. The first mention of the created nature of man and woman. This text is the first and foundational rule to sexuality. It is a theology of archetypes and firsts and design, where God defines gender, marriage and family, and sexual relations. Let's look at this creation intent.

What is so beautiful about the Genesis 1–3 narratives is they must be read together. From each of the works of God in creation through the ultimate creation of mankind in His image, when this narrative is read comprehensively, the coherence is stunning and can be clearly seen. For example, Genesis 1:26–28, the creation of humanity, and Genesis 2:7, 18–25 could be paraphrased like this:

> *"And God created humankind in His image. He created humankind as male and female. And God blessed them and told them to be fruitful and multiply.... Then God created human physically out of the dust of the earth and breathed into him and he came alive as Adam (meaning "of the earth").... As God watched Adam, He said that man should have a companion. So, He took a rib from the man Adam and created another human that Adam called woman. Therefore, a man shall leave his father and mother and be joined to his wife, and they shall become one flesh again."*

What a statement of the whole argument of gender, marriage, and sexual relations. We could end the discussion here. Yet, many of the writers and texts in the rest of the Bible will take us back here time and again.

Parenthetically, remember that later on, Genesis 5:1–22 retells the creation story by saying when God created them, He blessed them and called them *Adam*. "He gave this name both to the man and to the woman," according to Matthew Henry's *Complete Commentary*. This is a support of the archetype or first or design of humankind created as male and female in Genesis 1. But it wasn't until Genesis 2 that God breathed into the man *Adam*, and then put him to sleep and took his rib to create the woman *Adam (of the earth)*. She would not be renamed Eve until after the fall.

It is then in Genesis 3 where we pick up the story.

Through the temptation of Satan, we have the fall of the humans (Adams) in the garden of Eden and the resulting curse that God has for each of the players in this story. *Satan* is cursed as the tempter and lowest of all creation, and the enmity between him and humanity is set. The *woman (Adam)* is told her sorrow would be great in childbearing and that she would always have a desire for the man. The *man (Adam)* is then told that his labor would be a cursed earth and his work demanding.

It is finally after all of this that in their designed differences, Adam names the woman Eve.

> *We need to stop making the argument about sexuality more difficult than it is. Scripture has always come before culture. God spoke (Scripture) and creation (culture) happened. Whatever personal or cultural idea, teaching, or feeling has come after this scriptural definition and intent for gender, marriage, and sexuality is a deviation from the archetypical truth here in Genesis.*

There is no confusion on God's design and intent of male or female gender, marriage, or sexual relations in Scripture. There is no allowance in the Scriptures for nonbinary categories of a *third way*, *transition*, or *neutral* gender. No marriage consent outside of a husband and wife. And there is no unbounded free sexual behavior between men and women or same-sex relations.

In biblical cases of transgender or nonbinary language, and where marriage was not honored between a man and a woman and free sexual behavior was practiced, the Bible is clearly not condoning these things but merely speaking of their existence. Whether that included other mentions of eunuchs, a king taking multiple wives, rights of war, temple or otherwise prostitutes, and idolatrous or otherwise sexual relations, this foundational sexuality intent of Genesis is clear.

Four Intentions of Sexual Design

The simple understanding of this account in Genesis can be seen in four intentions of sexual design:

- A man and a woman were created as human.

- A man and a woman were created to perpetuate the human race within marriage.

- A man and a woman were created to experience naturally designed sex within marriage.

- A man and a woman were created to be a family that models human relations to God.

> *So, a proper theology of biblical sexuality includes the designation of male and female as human, procreation between a man and a woman in marriage, a designed natural sexual pleasure between the minds and bodies of a man and a woman in marriage, and a model of how family relates to God the Creator.*

Wow. That is inspiring. This is the first history of sexuality. The archetype.

It really is simple and doesn't need parsing. It is like math. One plus one always equals two. It did in 2020 BC and it does in AD 2020. Any culturally created substitute for this first order is not God's intent. Just because something becomes prevalent or popular in culture over time doesn't make it relevant or right. Just because the government legislates morality doesn't make it right. Each of us must see ourselves in the creation story and the ultimate design of God for our lives. Whatever replaces this Genesis intent of creation then becomes a substitute. An unnatural expression of sexuality.

When Teenagers Ask Questions

I love to talk to teenagers. Discussions with teenagers are unique, bizarre, intriguing, informative, mysterious, and rare at the same time. Young people can handle all kinds of topics and thoughts.

Recently, I was in Oregon and recorded a live podcast with teenagers on multiple topics ranging from the family and sexuality to faith, peers, culture, and apologetics. Every time I am with teenagers in forums like this, I walk away having learned so much about myself and young people. While doing the live podcast, a question regarding this Genesis text came up.

Lilith

One young lady asked a question about the first woman. But not Eve. What she was talking about was the creation account in Genesis 1 of mankind (Adam) representing both male and female, and another account in Genesis 2 of a helpmate so Adam wouldn't be alone. As we have said, these are simply two accounts that belong together in the creation of mankind originally and ultimately.

The *Midrash*—extra-biblical commentary and exegesis of Old Testament writings meant to sort through biblical thought—and Greek literature cite ancient beliefs that there was another female, Lilith, created before Eve. Lilith rebelled against Adam so God created Eve. In most of the Jewish traditions, the *Midrash* defines Lilith as a demon figure who did not want to be ruled by Adam. But the Lilith story is not consistent with Scripture. It falls under extra-biblical tradition.[14]

---

14. Joseph Dan, "Samael, Lilith, and the Concept of Evil in Early Kabbalah," *Association for Jewish Studies Review*, Vol. 5 (1980), 17–40 (www.jstor.org/stable/1486451?seq=1).

No one ever told me I shouldn't have sex before marriage,
but it seems like the right thing to do, you know?
—Carlee, age 16

PROVERBS 5–9

The second principle of sexuality can be found in Proverbs 5–9.

These texts are what I call *the wisdom intent*. This incredible run of writings from Solomon covers topics such as adultery, sexual wickedness, evil seduction, youthful lust, harlotry, real-life examples of immorality, and poor sexual judgment. The wisdom texts also talk about the dangers of sex outside of marriage. Wow. So much wisdom and safety in these chapters.

Boys, it's hypocritical to take something from a woman that
you don't want another man taking from your future wife.
—Jeanne Mayo, veteran youth leader

Look at the language of the writings of Solomon in these few chapters as he gives wisdom on how to turn from sexual sins:

- *The cost of adultery, fornication, and poor judgment is great*

- *How to preserve discretion in the heat of the moment*

- *Walking away from temptation*

- *The commands of your father and the law of your mother will guide you*

- *Don't lust after beauty*

- *The safety of understanding the way of sexual temptation*

- *Recognizing the spiral of enticing seductive speech*

- *The house of immorality is the house of hell*

- *Do not entertain the setting or the talk of adultery or fornication*

- *It is the simple who turn to sexual folly (whether from a lack of good sense or foolishness)*

In the midst of these words about sexuality, marriage, and sexual immorality, the solution is given in an overarching relationship of male and female. Solomon gives several escapes from the perils of adultery, sexual wickedness, evil seduction, youthful lust, harlotry, real-life examples of immorality, and poor sexual judgment. Solomon gives us insight into the cost of these mistakes, the power of the law and commandments, the advantage of understanding, and the escape of fleeing sexual sins from the perspective of male and female relationships. Does this not suggest an archetype of expected relational normality?

All of these wisdom sayings are wins if we practice Solomon's words. This is the ideal. The archetype. The design. The natural. The original. It just makes sense.

But above these wins, Solomon gives a powerful overarching design and default to our sexual fulfillment with these instructions:

> Do you know the saying, "Drink from your own rain barrel, draw water from your own spring-fed well"? It's true. Otherwise, you may one day come home and find your barrel empty and your well polluted. Your spring water is for you and you only, not to be passed around among strangers. Bless your fresh-flowing fountain! Enjoy the wife you married as a young man! Lovely as an angel, beautiful as a rose—don't ever quit taking delight in her body. Never take her love for granted! (Proverbs 5:15–19)

Wow. What a fantastic description of the power of love and sex from Solomon.

Before my wife passed, I remember reading these texts together. What a sexual design for Jane and me. And for every married couple. We were two different people when we met. But then something began to happen. She trusted me and I honored her as we began to date. And then, after I asked her father for her hand in marriage, we walked together for a year as we began to plan our wedding and subsequent married life.

On the day of our wedding, we held hands and gave ourselves to each other spiritually. That night after I locked the door behind us, she trusted me with not only her soul but her body. What came out of that union was unmatched and complete love, trust, and satisfaction. To this day, as a result of that union, I have three beautiful children and six grandchildren (and still counting).

> *Solomon, the wisest man to ever live, solves the problem of sexual folly in all of its forms as monogamous, exciting, emotional, graphic, and committed sexual relations between a man and his wife within marriage.*

There is no other description, or practice, that leaves humanity as stunned as this design. By the time you are done reading this account in the Proverbs as well as the Song of Solomon, there is no confusion, filthiness, warning, or ambiguity about sexuality.

- Sexuality and sex within marriage between a man and a woman is the *pinnacle.*

- Sexuality and sex within marriage between a man and a woman is *complementary.*

- Sexuality and sex within marriage between a man and a woman is *sensitive and strong.*

- Sexuality and sex within marriage between a man and a woman is the *perfect fit spiritually and physically.*

- Sexuality and sex within marriage between a man and a woman is the purest *form of earthly human love*.

- Sexuality and sex within marriage between a man and woman is the *climax*.

> *Sexuality and sex within marriage between a man and woman is the archetype of God's design for humanity, from Genesis through Revelation, and He wouldn't have it any other way. When this relationship ideal is right, every other sexual expression will be also.*

The best way to recognize the fake versions of sexuality we see thanks to *the Abagnale Effect* is to completely know the genuine sexuality of Scripture. We cannot spend more time looking at a faux sexuality in culture and expect to clearly see the real thing. This is why the spiraling biblical illiteracy in the Millennial and Gen Z sets is so disturbing. With a declining biblical worldview in the last two generations, we are seeing a popular counterfeit sexuality rise in its place. It can be easy to accept a falsehood when the truth is an unknown.

It is clear the entire biblical record promotes the same thing concerning gender, marriage, and sex as the monogamous sexual relations between a man and a woman within marriage. It is the default of Scripture. It is not our right to try to fit the cultural order of any time in history or our personal ideology into the Bible. Over and over again, from Genesis to Revelation, we are reminded the biblical model of all sexuality is a standardization. I know we don't like the term standardization in our culture today, but as Solomon reminds us in Proverbs and his Song, the norm for sexual relations is finding joy in the spouse of your youth. (See Proverbs 5:18.)

This early youthful relationship is not worth throwing away. Sometimes the first love relationship is unforgettable and lasting like Solomon describes here.

The reason I choose to keep my virginity for my wife is
because sex is a gift from God and I don't want to
throw that away for a moment of pleasure.
—Caleb, age 18

MATTHEW 5, 15, 19

The third principle of biblical sexuality is found in the New Testament.

This text is what I call *the Matthew intent*, or *the messianic intent*. Many people say Jesus had nothing to say about sexuality. That is far from the truth as we will see here and later in Jesus's words in Revelation. With His words, Jesus continues the creation intent of male and female, defining the natural family order, and placing sexual relations within marriage between a man and a woman.

Jesus does this by quoting Moses from the Genesis account and intention of the Creator. Asked about divorce, He said:

> Haven't you read in your Bible that the Creator originally made man and woman for each other, male and female? And because of this, a man leaves father and mother and is firmly bonded to his wife, becoming one flesh—no longer two bodies but one.
>
> (Matthew 19:4–6)

Jesus didn't feel the need to change the wording thousands of years and many generations later. Same language. And every other writer in the New Testament, when dealing with sexuality, includes some of the same words, using the common default order of creation with the male and female genders and biblical definitions of sexual immorality.

> *Jesus is quoting the Old Testament words of Moses from Genesis. Isn't that interesting? Jesus could have **evolved**. He could have **adjusted** to His day. Kind of like we do. But His definition of sexuality was taken from the creation or Genesis intent. Jesus didn't feel the need to change with the times and so He reaffirms Moses's words and resets very clearly what is going on in His culture with the creation intent.*

This is why I say that *culture* is changing but Scripture is *consistent*. To understand this principle, let's look at the language of Jesus and Paul in Scripture by using some of the words from earlier in this chapter.

The Greek Word *Porneia*

This is one of the reoccurring words Jesus used in the New Testament, specifically in the Gospel of Matthew. *Porneia* is the most common word used in the New Testament for sexual sins and mostly it has a broader meaning rather than a focused one. A combined definition of *porneia* would include *fornication or sexual uncleanness such as unchastity, sexual immorality, idolatry, illicit sexual intercourse, impurity, and selling off or surrendering virginity*.[15] Fornication is also used in the plural sense as the collection of multiple sexual sins.

> Virginity is no longer gold to protect but rather a prize to be collected by the opposite sex.
> —Whitney Tellez, youth pastor

You may say that Jesus never said anything against sex before marriage, or He never said anything about incest, bestiality, prostitution, or homosexuality. Let's be very clear. When Matthew quotes Jesus as using the word *porneia*, like most of the other writers

15. David Janzen, "The Meaning of Porneia in Matthew 5.32 and 19.9: an Approach From the Study of Ancient Near Eastern Culture," *Journal for the Study of the New Testament*, March 2001 (theosophical.files.wordpress.com/2015/02/porneia-in-mt-5_32-and-19_9-janzen.pdf).

in the New Testament, He was using it in reference to a plurality of sexual issues. Several theologians from varying backgrounds speak to this broad use of the word:

- Colin Brown, professor emeritus of systematic theology at Fuller Seminary, said *porneia* "can describe various extra-marital sexual modes of behavior *insofar as they deviate from accepted social and religious norms* (e.g. homosexuality, promiscuity, pedophilia, and especially prostitution)."[16]

- Verlyn David Verbrugge wrote, "Rabbinical Judaism frowned on any kind of prostitution or extramarital sexual intercourse. Incest and all other kinds of unnatural sexual intercourse were viewed clearly as *porneia*."[17]

- The *Exegetical Dictionary of the New Testament* states that *porneia* means *"prostitution, unchastity, fornication,"* and is used *"of every kind of unlawful sexual intercourse."* Since Paul clearly alludes to homosexuality as sexual immorality in Romans 1, *porneia* also refers to homosexuality as sexual immorality.[18]

- Gerhard Kittel, one of the most respected theologians and lexicographers on this topic, said *porneia* includes *"unnatural adultery, fornication, licentiousness, and homosexuality."*[19]

The Greek Word *Arsenokoitai*

Paul wrote quite a bit about the topic of sexuality. In 1 Corinthians 6:9, he uses the compound Greek word *arsenokoitai*, meaning *arseno*, or the word for "a male," and *koitai*, or the word for "mat" or "bed." Put the two halves together and the word means *a male bed* or a

---

16. Colin Brown, *Dictionary of New Testament Theology*, Vol. 1 (Grand Rapids, MI: Zondervan, 1975).
17. Ibid.
18. Horst Balz and Gerhard Schneider, *Exegetical Dictionary of the New Testament* (Grand Rapids, MI: Eerdmans Publishing Company, 1993).
19. Gerhard Kittel, *Theological Dictionary of the New Testament* (Grand Rapids, MI: Eerdmans Publishing Company, 1976).

person who makes use of a *male-only bed* or a *bed for males*. Also, the Greek *koitai* is the source of the English word *coitus,* or "sexual intercourse." The conclusion is that the word *arsenokoitai* is referring to homosexuals who are in bed with other men, engaging in same-gender sexual activity.

A popular argument among progressives is that this word is only about the active role player in the relationship and what Paul really meant here was *pederasty,* or when older men took younger men or boys for pleasure. However, if this were true, Paul could have easily used the word for this practice: *paiderastis.*

There are other arguments against the clarity of this word, but here are some very clear points made by respected theologian Robert Gagnon:

- To broaden the word *arsenokoitai* to include exploitive heterosexual intercourse appears unlikely in view of the unqualified nature of the Levitical prohibitions.

- In every instance in which the *arsenokoit* word group occurs in a context that offers clues as to its meaning—that is, beyond mere inclusion in a vice list—it denotes homosexual intercourse.

- The term *arsenokoitai* itself indicates an inclusive sense of all men who play the active role in homosexual intercourse. Had Paul intended to single out pederasts, he could have used the technical term *paiderastïs.*

- The meaning that Paul gave to *arsenokoitai* has to be unpacked in light of Romans 1:24–27. When Paul speaks of the sexual intercourse of *"men with men"* (*arsenes en arsenes*) in verse 27, he obviously has *arsenokoitai* in mind.[20]

---

20. Robert A. J. Gagnon, *The Bible and Homosexual Practice: Texts and Hermeneutics* (Nashville, TN: Abingdon Press, 2001).

WHAT JESUS SAID ABOUT SEXUALITY

Here are a few things to consider concerning Jesus's words on sexuality:

First of all, Jesus's statements about gender, marriage, and sexual immorality in Matthew 5, 15, and 19—and later in Revelation, as we will see—overrides all of the other sexual offenses you can think of in one phrase. To be even broader, look at John 8 and the story of the woman caught in adultery and brought before Jesus. Jesus was clearly stating that adultery was a sin and that sex outside of marriage between a man and a woman was a sin—because He told her to not sin anymore! Of course, Jesus supported the woman who was caught in adultery; He showed her kindness publicly, and then He simply said to her, *"Go on your way. From now on, don't sin"* (verse 11).

Second, look at this thought from these messianic texts. Jesus clearly defines binary *gender* as male and female, *marriage* between a man and woman, and *sexual relations* outside of marriage between a man and a woman as *sinful* (His words, not mine). If you read these texts in Matthew, you will see how Jesus felt about all of this.

Third, just because Jesus may not have addressed a topic directly by using a certain word we are looking for—a word that did not exist at the time because there were other words like *porneia* that covered all sorts of sexual immorality—does that mean any other authors in the Bible (Moses, Solomon, Paul, Peter, Jude, or John) who may have addressed that topic hold a lesser authority for us? Of course not.

Fourth, it is clear that Jewish culture was very much against sex outside of marriage, incest, bestiality, and homosexual relations. How would it sound if Jesus and the other authors went around speaking often of those things to the Jews if they were not commonly accepted practices? Jewish culture understood this completely. It was Roman culture prior to Christ that had a more progressive view of sexual immorality. This is partly why Christ's message on these behaviors was succinct. Besides, Paul had such a dynamic role to play with the Romans, the message of sexual purity was definitely getting across.

Finally, because words carried multiple meanings in the Jewish culture, Jesus entered the discussion on and used the general words for incest, bestiality, prostitution, or homosexuality indirectly and directly by speaking of the principle of sex within marriage. These unnatural and prohibited behaviors were addressed by Jesus because the word He used was inclusive of all of these.

I believe Jesus was so clear on His stance regarding sexual prohibitions that He did not feel the need to address other sexual sins or evils directly because they were included in His broadly covered statement.

> *To use these practical points in a modern setting, say a police officer pulls me over and tells me I was driving 62 in a 55 mph zone, so he gives me a ticket. My argument cannot be that I did not break the law because the president did not tell me this, or because I have always driven a few miles over the speed limit and nobody else stopped me, or it wasn't clearly posted and I did not see the sign.*

The application of the principle became binding when the Holy Spirit inspired the biblical writers to include it.

I'd like to mention one more thing regarding the messianic intent.

In Matthew 15, when Jesus talks to the scribes and Pharisees about what defiles a person, He uses the word *porneia*, which, as we have seen in all of our translations, includes sexual immorality or intercourse. By using that word, Jesus is prohibiting all sexual relations outside of marriage between a man and a woman. That is very clear and inclusive. Defilement of the design was His main point. This is partly why we can advocate for someone who may be tempted by homosexuality to remain celibate and not give in to the act.

In fact, Jesus had enough to say about sexual immorality. He was just very succinct on the matter. We will cover what Jesus said in Revelation on the subject in a later chapter.

When we wander from the original messianic biblical intent, we create secondary unnatural order, a *cultural* order and not a *scriptural* order. This is what creates the problems we have in culture today. And the problems created outside of God's boundaries are many. Thus, whatever replaces the Genesis intent or the wisdom intent or the Matthew intent then becomes a substitute breaking from the original biblical intent.

LOOKING AT OTHER SCRIPTURES

ROMANS 1

Paul was very familiar with the New Testament world, especially Rome and Corinth. Context matters. The Roman Empire was the ruling system at the beginning of Jesus's ministry and its culture was sexually progressive. But it was tyrannical and oppressive; the people in the Mediterranean region were restless. Aside from being Caesar-led, the Roman government did not like Jesus or His followers because they were upsetting the region with a new movement. Most of Jesus's message was not appreciated.

The problems were growing between Rome and the Hellenists or Greeks. The Romans became even more liberal and graphic than the Greeks in everything from the arts and literature to sexuality. It was into this society that the message of Christ and His followers came.

The stand Paul made in his letter to the Romans represented a huge cultural shift.

We are faced with the same decision that Paul faced in the first century, writing his letter to the Romans. Are we going to stand against the sexual revolution that is rising in America? What we are facing today is a problem we have not corrected for decades. How will our stand look in relation to Paul's?

Argument of Design and Idolatry

In Romans 1, we have the ultimate of a degenerative loss of God's design of sexuality in Scripture. And Paul gave no ground.

> *Refusing to know God, they soon didn't know how to be human either—women didn't know how to be women, men didn't know how to be men. Sexually confused, they abused and defiled one another, women with women, men with men—all lust, no love. And then they paid for it, oh, how they paid for it—emptied of God and love, godless and loveless wretches.* (Romans 1:26–27)

One of the most accurate reviews of Romans 1 on the topic of sexuality was done by Dr. Robert A. J. Gagnon, a professor of New Testament Theology at Houston Baptist University. Gagnon has received accolades and respect from both sides of the sexuality argument as one of the foremost interpreters on the subject of human sexuality.

Look at Gagnon's clarity on the significance of Paul's statements regarding sexuality:

> Jews and Christians recognized that the scriptural understanding of human sexuality was not accessible only to those who had exposure to the Scriptures of the Jews. Since the Creator had designed human sexual pairing for

complementary "sexual others," it is not surprising that such a design was imbedded in compatible opposite-sex differences and still observable in the natural world set in motion by the Creator's decree. Hence, Paul could argue in Romans 1:24–27 that even Gentiles without access to Scripture had enough knowledge in creation/nature to know that same-sex unions represented a non-complementary sexual pairing, an "unnatural" union, a violation of Creator's will for creation. The naturalness of opposite-sex unions is readily visible in the areas of anatomy, physiology—that is, the procreative capacity—and in a host of interpersonal aspects.... To tamper with that naturalness and to act as if male-female sexual differences are not vital components of sexual pairings is, in short, to reap the whirlwind. There is no disharmony between Scripture and nature on this score.[21]

Romans 1 then is speaking of the spiral downward or the degeneration of the original design of sexuality in creation and nature. Some will say this chapter is only about idolatry in sexual immorality. My answer to that is yes. And. Both. The focus is not simply on idolatry; the focus is upon outcomes of idolatry—committing shameful acts and exchanging the original natural creation use of the body for sex with the unnatural and idolatrous use of sex. Whether or not idolatry was involved, Paul says it is still unnatural.

> *God's natural revelation, which testifies to the existence of God as the Supreme Designer, includes the compatibility and complementarity of the male/female union. As idolatry corrupts God's revelation, homosexuality itself is seen as being one of the blasphemous manifestations of idolatry, a turning away from God's natural order.*

21. Interview with Robert A. J. Gagnon, "Scripture on Homosexuality," ZENIT (www.catholicfidelity.com/apologetics-topics/morality/scripture-on-homosexuality-by-robert-a-j-gagnon).

What is clear in this text is that the people of the region—Romans, Greeks, and Gentiles—had no excuse for not following the creation order. A *natural* understanding of human sexuality was clearly seen in God's creative design of complementary bodies for relationship and sex. Not just the parts or the observable pleasure of the parts fitting together during sex, but the mental and emotional compatibility of opposite-sex design. Furthermore, since the beginning of time, sex outside of marriage between a man and a woman has been considered unnatural.

PAUL IN HIS LETTERS OR EPISTLES

Paul continues his words in his letters to the churches in the Roman Empire.

GALATIANS 5; 1 CORINTHIANS 6-7

Since we have already mentioned the culture of the Roman Empire in the Mediterranean region, let's go specifically to the language in the words that Paul chooses.

Paul uses some of the same language addressing our sexual behavior as Jesus did. However, Paul adds something very important to the discussion. Paul talks of *patterns* and *practices*; he places great emphasis on sustained or patterned behavior. Paul speaks strongly against illicit sexual relations, referring to adultery, fornication, unnatural lewdness, a soft, effeminate male submitting to unnatural relations, a male who lies with a male, *and things like these!* These words include prostitution, rape, pederasty (older men having sex with younger boys), and idolatry. You cannot limit meanings to words that are used. What is clear in Paul's language is the broad coverage of sexual promiscuity.

One of the things Paul was known for was his lists. He loved to be clear by creating lists. We will get into more detail later on in the book also, but his epistles are very clear.

> In the epistles, Paul brings together patterns and death and comes to a powerful conclusion: our sins are not to be taken lightly, they are to be taken to the cross. It's almost as if Paul felt a responsibility to clean up the entire Roman Empire with very practical language in the epistles. Paul's call to holiness was real. No doubt, as C. S. Lewis said, "Paul was the greatest Christian to ever live."

The Concept of Flesh

Maybe Paul's greatest contribution to Christianity is the concept of death to the flesh. This contribution placed major emphasis for the first century—and for you and me—to consider our behavior. Because Paul talked about dying so much, it is clear he was saying human sexuality is so strong that we must not be mastered by it.

On more than one occasion, Paul spoke of the battle between the spirit and the flesh, saying they are contrary to each other. "*There is a root of sinful self-interest in us that is at odds with a free spirit*" (Galatians 5:17).

> So much of what I hear people justifying in their life sounds like "I just feel this way," or, "If God didn't want me to desire this, He would take my desire away." But what we have forgotten is our own responsibility to deny ourselves and not just rely on God's deliverance. God certainly can **deliver** us from some things, but we must also be **disciplined** from these things!

Furthermore, Paul states in 1 Corinthians 6:12, *"Just because something is technically legal doesn't mean that it's spiritually appropriate. If I went around doing whatever I thought I could get by with, I'd be a slave to my whims."* If you read the context, Paul is not just talking about food here, as some argue. Because Paul's next statement addresses this other list of fleshly behaviors and specifically sexual immorality. In other words, the point of living is not about trying to get away with everything we can in life, but to understand God's intent for our lives. These intents are given to us through the Bible and they are not to be bartered away or traded for personal standardization.

In Galatians 5:13, Paul is using similar language when he states, *"It is absolutely clear that God has called you to a free life. Just make sure that you don't use this freedom as an excuse to do whatever you want to do and destroy your freedom."* A few verses later, he lists patterns or practices of sinful behaviors, noting, *"If you use your freedom this way, you will not inherit God's kingdom"* (verse 21).

I believe this is an important point. Just because we feel a certain way or have been told we are a certain way doesn't mean that we are to submit to this. Our feelings have nothing to do with our identity. God's spiritual words over us are more important than our fleshly feelings about us.

> We don't have a gender confusion problem. We have an identity problem. When we realize our identity in Christ, confusion will disappear.
> —Graham Betancourt, youth pastor

CONSENSUAL HOMOSEXUALITY

One of the common arguments in the modern gay movement is that the Bible was not speaking about the conditions of consensual homosexuality as we see it today. In other words, it is okay to have loving, committed, same-sex relationships without rape, prostitution, idolatry, or lust.

Think about that. The notion that *some* homosexual relationships are acceptable—or, for that matter, some gossip, some prejudice, some idolatry, or some addictions—if they are consensual and loving? That concept cannot be found in Paul's writing at all. He wasn't built that way.

I might add, this theology is not *a push for heterosexual sex*. That has its own stains. In his book *Holy Sexuality and the Gospel*, Christopher Yuan says, "Heterosexuality isn't the ideal. Unless it is faithful in marriage or chastity in singleness."[22] This is a great reminder that just because God designed us to have hetero sex does not mean it should take place outside of faithfulness in marriage.

FINALLY

Enough for now on the theology of sexuality. We will deal with more theology from several other writers and several other texts with more views on human sexuality in a chapter covering *tough questions* at the end of the book. We will bring in more theology on sexuality from Jesus's thoughts as well as Jude from his brief but powerful letter and John's words from Revelation. I hope you find the format in that chapter more practical and easier to apply.

With all of the definitions we have covered in this one, remember to use this information to create your box or framework to shape your thinking on sexuality. See if this information can help you to shape your worldview on sexuality. I would encourage you to read this chapter one more time. I think it will help you process what the Holy Spirit is saying to you.

---

22. Christopher Yuan, *Holy Sexuality and the Gospel: Sex, Desire, and Relationships Shaped by God's Grand Story* (Colorado Springs, CO: Multnomah Press, 2018).

And remember, this information is *not* about winning arguments, or who is right and who is wrong. It is about understanding, as clearly as we can, scriptural principles rather than cultural norms and feelings. Be careful not to win arguments and lose friendships.

There is no dignity when the human dimension is eliminated from the person. In short, the problem with pornography is not that it shows too much of the person, but, that it shows far too little of the person.   —Pope John Paul II

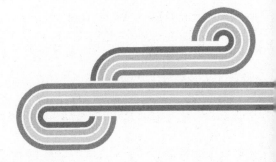

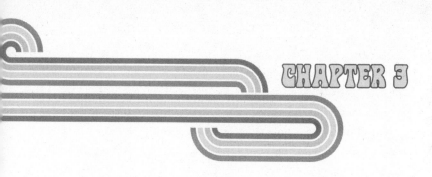

A TEENAGER'S GREATEST WIN

The Hookup

A teenager's greatest win may be keeping their virginity as they navigate through the present sexual revolution going on in America today. One of the current topics in teen and young adult sexual behavior is called *the hookup*. These are casual relationships with *no strings attached*.

Maybe the easiest way to demonstrate this "no strings attached" encounter is to look at the evolution of this analogy.

> *A few years back, the **hookup** meant something entirely different than what it means today. My grandpa would **hook up** the trailer and haul a load of something. My dad would **hook up** the antenna on the rooftop so we could watch TV. I used to **hook up** with my friends and go out for pizza after a football game on Friday night. Today, this generation will **hook up** with someone and assume a high-risk, flirting, no strings attached/ no big deal evening of sex, with no obligation afterwards. We've come a long way from **hooking up** trailers or the TV antenna, or going out with friends for pizza after a game.*

There is no doubt that one of the central issues in adolescent life is sexuality. I have stated for years that the family is the most important issue in a teenager's life. (We will cover the subject of family and sexuality in-depth in chapter five.) You could argue for the breakdown of the family or social media or even peer influence as central issues in a teenager's life. But few would disagree with the enormous influence of this present sexual revolution on teenagers in our society today.

NEW TERRITORY

The sexual revolution we are going through can be clearly seen in another obvious change in our culture: the language and linguistics surrounding the sexual identity types. A quick search on the Internet will reveal literally dozens of new sexuality terms coined for a new generation of Millennials and Gen Z.

The Faculty of Medicine at the University of Toronto advises:

> Don't try and fit people into a mold. Pay attention to people's language. Much variability exists and terminology is ever-changing. People have the right to describe their gender and sexuality however they choose.[23]

Sure, but this does not change the truth of Scripture. The latest run of letters and numbers added to the identity spectrum is telling. We should be aware of these new terms and feel comfortable talking about these so we are able to understand where people are coming from.

LGBTTQQIP2SAA (often abbreviated as LGBTQ+) is only a partial list of the dozens of new terms:

- Lesbian – Sexually attracted to women

- Gay – Sexually attracted to men

---

23. LGBT infographic, University of Toronto Faculty of Medicine (thehub.utoronto.ca/family/wp-content/uploads/2018/03/LGBT-Infographic.pdf).

- Bisexual – Sexually attracted to both

- Transgender – Does not identify with birth sex

- Transsexual – Transitioning from one sex to another

- Queer – Sexual gender minorities

- Questioning – Unsure and exploring

- Intersex – Not distinctly male or female

- Pansexual – Sexually attracted to any identity

- Two-spirit – Gender-variant Indigenous person

- Asexual – Low or no attraction to anyone

- Ally – Does not identify to LGBTQ+ but sympathizes or supports

Additionally, some of those who categorize themselves as one of these genders prefer neutral or alternate pronouns. These include "them" rather than him or her, and "ze" rather than he or she. Most of the progressive liberals would agree that gender, sex, and sexuality are intertwined concepts, but distinct from one another. In other words, you cannot place someone's sexual attraction solely based on their gender identity anymore. What *is* true is we are not living in your grandmother's world anymore—to be honest, we are not living in your parents' world either.

Given the moment our youth culture is in right now, you will see there is a demand in this book.

This book demands that the greatest impact a generation could have on their contemporaries is to help solve the worst of its problems. The problems in the youth culture today are many, including family, media, identity, anxiety, self-harm, mental health, school violence, and the sexual revolution. Let's see if we can help solve the sexual revolution as we walk through this book.

TEEN SEXUAL BEHAVIOR

> Every time we have sex with someone,
> a piece of our soul goes with them.
> —Graham Betancourt, youth pastor

How do teenagers navigate the tsunami of sexuality crashing over their lives? How do they navigate the waters of gender fluidity, the redefinition of marriage, and the sexually illicit hookup era? Could it be the greatest mark Gen Z could have on their world is to bring a return to traditional biblical values in sexuality? Will Gen Z be able to help their generation build a new sexuality box?

We've already seen some interesting numbers concerning sexuality and young people. Here are a few more:

- The percentage of singles is on the rise (30 percent)

- Gen Z is more cautious and less risk-averse

- More than half of Millennials feel that teen sex is okay (54 percent)

- Almost three-quarters of adults think teens waiting for sex is a higher priority (71 percent)

- Practicing Christians believe strongly teens should wait for sex (96 percent)

- Adults who have no faith are much less stringent on teens waiting for sex (28 percent)

- Gen Z having sex in high school has decreased from 1991 (55 percent) to today (51 percent)

- Faith is the single most powerful factor in determining whether and when to have sex[24]

Researchers have found that Gen Z's *personal* use of technology to access the Internet has delayed their *public* desire for dating

---

24. Barna Group, *Barna Trends 2018*.

relationships. However, this has increased their sexual output through sexting, Tinder and Grindr soft porn searches, and self-sex. So, statistically, Gen Z is having fewer traditional relationship experiences such as dating, but more virtual and online sex.

Here is how Nosheen Iqbal of *The Guardian* describes Gen Z and their unique traits:

> They drink less, take far fewer drugs, and have made teen-age pregnancy a near anomaly. Generation Z—one of several terms used to describe post-millennial youth born after 1996—prefer juice bars to pub crawls, rank quality family time ahead of sex and prioritize good grades before friendship.[25]

I believe Iqbal captures the Gen Z trait quite well. Their initiative, industry, and competitive educational nature seems to drive most of them above sexually elicit relationships...yet at the same time, they are more active sexually in other ways. Certainly, given these findings, Gen Z is going to redefine sexuality for their set. What that looks like will be determined largely by their families and youth leaders who can communicate a clear faith-objective for sexuality to teenagers and young people today.

What is evident in the statistics and research among teenagers is their courtesy toward sexuality in general. This definitely relates to their loss of theology as we will see throughout this book. Because Gen Z only has a 4 percent biblical worldview, they have taken their sexuality ethic from culture instead of Scripture. This generous grace is something other generations did not display relationally to the area of sexuality. This generous attitude toward others and their sexuality is a beautiful picture of Christ, even though it may seem to lack the truth of biblical sexuality.

25. Nosheen Iqbal, "Generation Z: 'We have more to do than drink and take drugs,'" *The Guardian*, July 21, 2018 (www.theguardian.com/society/2018/jul/21/generation-z-has-different-attitudes-says-a-new-report).

This is why I believe grace could be a part of our faith conversation to lead Gen Z back to a theological construct or box.

In its Ipsos Thinks report *Beyond Binary: The Lives and Choices of Generation Z*, the London-based market research firm Ipsos MORI says:

> There is some indication that growing up in a more accepting society has had an impact on how young people view sexuality more generally. For example, among British school children, three in five (60%) of 15-16 year olds think sexuality is a scale and that it is possible to be somewhere in the middle. Self-identification among older UK Generation Z (16-22) seems to follow a similar pattern: just two thirds (66%) think of themselves as exclusively attracted to the opposite sex, compared with 71% of Millennials, 85% of Gen X and 88% of Baby Boomers.[26]

The research firm also reports:

> Similar to their opinions on sexuality, Generation Z seem to see a spectrum of gender identities – with evidence that gender neutrality is more of a norm among young people than it was for Millennials. In 2016 in the US, three quarters (74%) of Generation Z (13-20) said they are more accepting of nontraditional gender identities than they were a year ago – compared with 64% of younger Millennials (21-27). And well over half (56%) said they knew someone who uses non-gender-binary terms (they/them/ze etc.), compared with 47% of younger Millennials (21-27) and 43% of older Millennials (28-34).[27]

"In particular, this generation of young has grown up at a time when gender as a simple binary and fixed identity has been questioned

26. Bobby Duffy et al, *Beyond Binary: The Lives and Choices of Generation Z*, August 2018 (www.ipsos.com/ipsos-mori/en-uk/ipsos-thinks-beyond-binary-lives-and-choices-generation-z).
27. Ibid.

much more widely," Hannah Shrimpton, one of the authors of the report, told the *Daily Telegraph*. "This is new, and will affect wider views of gender, sexuality and much broader aspects of identity."[28]

For decades, sociologists have tried to explain teen behavior. I mean, all of culture has tried to explain teen behavior at some point—without success. It's like trying to hold water in your hand. You think you have it, but it slips between your fingers.

FACTORS SHAPING TEENAGE SEXUALITY

So what are the factors contributing to adolescent sexuality development? To be honest, that is an easy answer. Because it is a composite answer. Anyone who tells you it is one thing may not really understand young people. I believe the sexuality formation of teenagers is broad and would include their home, peers, social groups, society, religion, music, media, physiology, ethnicity, neighborhood geography, and even their schools or education.

Let's take a quick look at a few of these contributors to teen sexuality development. If we are going to help teenagers win in their sexual lives, we will have to address the following.

RELIGION (CHRISTIANITY)

The second chapter on the theology of love and sexuality defines this in detail, but let me include faith here with a few additional thoughts.

It doesn't matter if a young person is churched or unchurched; they are going to be raised in America with some measure of faith development. It happens through many of the sectors of society, both formally and informally, biblically and non-biblically. If the religious upbringing of an adolescent is not based in Christianity or the Bible,

---

28. Olivia Rudgard, "Only two thirds of Generation Z identify as 'exclusively heterosexual,'" *Daily Telegraph*, July 5, 2018 (www.telegraph.co.uk/news/2018/07/05/two-thirds-generation-z-identify-exclusively-heterosexual).

their faith development will come in another form, even if it is amoral codes derived from culture and society.

How do we improve the impact of Christianity in a teenager's life? It will take the church to show up in the life of the teen world with a biblically-based, authentic, counterculture of principle and grace. Gen Z already is thinking differently about sexuality. And although their viewpoints may not be biblical, they do allow for a lot of grace.

Teenagers today are diverse in their civil rights and inclusive in their sexual rights. Gen Z today is totally comfortable with friends who may not hold the conservative or classic view of sexuality. In fact, seven out of ten teens think it is acceptable to be born one gender and feel like another. And 35 percent say they know someone who is nonbinary.[29]

Do you see the grace of God in the research?

What has already been proven is the importance of faith as a contributing factor for a teenager developing their view of sexuality. Of course, this seems odd given the theological vacuum of this generation. But I think this also speaks to the power of the truth of God placed in every person at creation when He breathed into us. I see this relational grace in our teenagers as a perfect avenue to introduce them to Christ, His love, and His plan for their life. The grace they display is God's grace in them!

It simply needs some truth filtered into the grace.

CULTURE

As we will see completely in the next chapter, culture is a powerful force.

Culture can be seen in political, entertainment, corporate, recreational, local/global, or even marketing and advertising sectors. Culture is the

29. Samantha Allen, "Over a Third of Generation Z Knows a Non-Binary Person," *Daily Beast*, Jan. 24, 2019 (www.thedailybeast.com/over-a-third-of-generation-z-knows-a-non-binary-person).

thinking, language, codes, ways, beliefs, and behaviors of a specific group or subgroup. This cultural DNA around us may be the most influential constant in all of our lives. In this information age, we cannot escape culture in any setting, but the culture in the teenage setting is highly influential because of the ease with which it can create popular feeling, thought, and ultimately action in an adolescent's life.

> *The culture in American teen life today encourages hypersensitivity regarding social status: comparing one's self to everyone else, obsessing over who to sit with in the lunchroom, whether to date or not, freaking out over what to wear at school each day, and even what phone to get. Culture is unrelenting.*

Aside from these considerations, culture is even more powerful when it comes to sexuality. It is a cultural tsunami crashing over teens and sweeping them away in its powerful wave. The teen sexual culture is driven by the obsessive market researchers, trendsetters, and cool hunters who force their ideas on teenagers—telling them how they should look, what they should wear, the kind of behavior permissible on a date, or even personal boundaries for pornography. This kind of progressive sexual culture is pervasive and overwhelming to teenagers. Especially if they are not grounded in a biblical framework of sexuality.

It almost seems impossible for a teenager to win against the sensual culture of sexuality in America. In the face of this unrelenting environment, it is important that we help teenagers to find the truth. If we do this, they will be able to stand against this in-your-face eroticism in America with a powerful combination of grace and truth. This should not be difficult because since the beginning of time, dating back to creation, there is an undeniable witness of Christianity in all things.

If we can help young people to see this, it will help Gen Z solve their peers' greatest problem.

Here's another influential contributor to teen sexuality.

MEDIA

It all began quietly about twenty-five years ago, but everything took an ominous turn in the past ten years. Television and mass media are now bedfellows that are changing viewership. The Internet, email, MySpace, Facebook, smartphones, Twitter, YouTube, Instagram, Snapchat, TikTok, and the countless websites and apps for social networking and gaming are now available in our hands, on our wrist, or seen through an eyeglass lens. Who would have thought that social platforms, apps, trivia games, or crossword puzzles would be a way to stay in touch with people, get our news, pay our bills, bully others, or do sexting? Look at a few findings on the power of media in a teen's life:

- In a study of youth ages thirteen and fourteen, heavy exposure to sexually oriented television drastically increased their acceptance of nonmarital sex.[30]

- A Kaiser Family Foundation study showed that when those ages twelve to seventeen are exposed to heavy sexual content on TV, it accelerates their initiation of sexual intercourse and other advanced sexual activities.[31]

- The American Psychological Association estimates that each year, teenagers are exposed to 14,000 sexual references and innuendoes on television.

Gen Z needs boundaries and balance with parents who will support and guide them processing life versus destroying their initiative
—Whitney Tellez, youth pastor

30. Barna Group, *Gen Z.*
31. Dale Kunkel, et al, *Sex on TV 2005: A Kaiser Family Foundation Report* (www.kff.org/wp-content/uploads/2013/01/sex-on-tv-4-full-report.pdf).

Whether they are on their phone, watching television, listening to a song, viewing a sporting event, or playing a video game, teenagers are exposed to unrealistic body image expectations. This distorts their definition of self and gives them false beliefs about their sexuality and appearance. With size zero held up as an ideal—the average fashion model is thinner than 98 percent of American women—it's no wonder that 81 percent of ten-year-olds are afraid of being fat.[32]

All of this can lead to *the law of diminishing returns*—the idea that what may move us or fulfill us initially takes much more effort over time. For example, maybe just thinking of someone gave you goosebumps at one time, but that no longer is the case. Now, you might need to speak to them face to face or touch them to get the same thrill. The longer the relationship, the smaller the return on investment.

> *Tom Reichert, a professor and researcher at the University of Georgia, notes that whereas a glimpse of an ankle might have been effective several generations ago, a greater degree of nudity is needed today to get the same result.* "**It takes more explicitness to grab our attention** *and arouse us than before," he says. "In the early 1900s, exposed arms and ankles of female models generated the same level of arousal as partially nude models do today. We can see during our lifetimes the changes in sexually explicit content on television, movies, books and other forms of media beyond just advertising.*"[33]

All of the sociological research models place teenagers on their mobile device around five to six hours a day, and in front of *all* screens (television, computer, and iPads) about nine to ten hours daily. These *screenagers* today spend more time on their phones

---

32. PBS, "Perfect Illusions: Eating Disorders and the Family" (www.pbs.org/perfectillusions/eatingdisorders/ preventing_facts.html).

33. April Reese Sorrow, "Magazine trends study finds increase in advertisements using sex," *UGA Today*, June 5, 2012 (news.uga.edu/magazine-trends-study-finds-increase-in-advertisements-using-sex).

but have fewer apps than their older brothers and sisters, the Millennials. We cannot stop this media wave crashing on our kids.

We cannot stop the rushing cultural train pushing forward with increasing speed, creativity, and power by simply holding up our ant-sized fist in protest. Rather than trying to halt this social force, it is much wiser to put our efforts into redeeming everything for the purposes of God. Teaching teens how to use their media for good. And understanding, ourselves, that these tools may be the easiest way to communicate the gospel to a digital generation in their own language.

SCHOOL

Family. Theology. Peers. Media. School. Wow, each of these are such formative sexuality influences in a teenager's life.

In a normal, non-pandemic world, a teenager will spend about thirty-five to forty hours at school weekly, depending on extracurricular activities. See the problem? There may not be a more formative framework in a teen's life. Whether that is seen in the peers who are with them, the progressive education they are receiving, or the lack of religion allowed in their development, the school campus is a formidable companion of teens. It is the one place that dominates most of a teen's life. At least by the measurement of time.

It touts great consistency and influence on relationships and sexuality. This is how the mainstream media, particularly the progressive magazine *Teen Vogue*, looks at the setting of the campus influence and the hookup culture:

> Despite the often-negative press, hookups, or, short term sexual/intimate encounters, like one-night stands, summer flings, and semester-long friends-with-benefits relationships, can come with a lot of descriptors: "casual," "fun," "random,"

and "spontaneous" can be some, but can they also be ethical, considerate, and satisfying? We think yes![34]

Of course, *Teen Vogue* would think illicit sexual relationships outside of marriage could be ethical. Because they would not have a biblical basis for stating what is or is not ethical. Their ethics are based on culture, not Scripture. This is why we talk about the difference between a *changing culture* and an *unchanging Scripture*. Of course, it is popular to practice illicit sexual relationships. But popularity does not prove principle. In any case, the hookup is a revolution to the Millennial and the Gen Z crowd that is propagated at school.

There is something to say about the six to seven hours daily a teenager will spend under the influence of the school system. Most teenagers have little say over the school they attend, their courses of study, or their classmates. These conditions give rise to more symbolic forms of thinking and behavior defined by a clash of worlds and belief systems. Principals, staff, teachers, peers, coaches, content material, and course offerings are constant companions in the daily life of a teenager.

Status systems are set in the school system.

At some point, we must be raising Gen Z with a theological boldness that prepares them for the school setting. Are they able to defend the faith? Are they able to define the faith? Do they have a strong enough set of principles to counter what I call *the campus code*? Codes are being set and ethics are being formed without the discipline of Scripture. There is a liberal and progressive ideology that our teenagers cannot escape.

As we read through the New Testament story of the work of Christ, it is remarkable that more miracles happened outside of the temple in the first century. Just in Mark 1–6, there are about twenty-six times

---

34. Yana Tallon-Hicks, "How to Be an Ethical Hookup Partner," *Teen Vogue*, August 12, 2019 (www.teenvogue.com/story/how-to-be-an-ethical-hook-up).

where Jesus was teaching, preaching, and working. We see Him in the marketplace, by the seashore, in a boat, on the countryside, up in the mountains, at a cemetery, at a sinner's home, and in His own home. In those first six chapters of Mark, Jesus was only found in the temple twice.

It was remarkable how Christ worked in the context of the people. We need the same commitment in youth ministry today. We need to help our students reset the status systems in the school system. If the incredible launch of Christianity in the first century began outside of the temple, then we must raise disciples who think the same way.

Standardization forces all kinds of thinking and behavior—and not just with sexuality. How do we improve the impact of schooling on a young person? We must emphasize the *supernatural* in the face of the *standardization* of ethics and codes. This generation loves the supernatural. It could be the supernatural that is able to rise up against the tsunami of sexuality our students face daily in school.

I'm reminded of a supernatural story I heard from a youth pastor in Ohio.

> *On Wednesday afternoon at football practice, one of the team's star players was injured and fell to the ground. It was a serious injury that stopped practice. The coaches called for the trainers and the trainers called for the EMTs and an ambulance was on the way. As the player was motionless on the ground, the position groups stopped around the field to watch what was going on.*
>
> *There were five young men on the football team who were part of the school's Fellowship of Christian Athletes leadership team. They went over to the injured student, took off their helmets, and knelt beside him in front of the whole team. As they prayed for the young man, he was healed. He*

> *sat up, moving around and emotional. Much to the dismay of*
> *the coaches and trainer.*
>
> *God had done an amazing miracle through the obedience*
> *of these students. The injured player got a doctor's note of*
> *clearance and played in his football game on Friday night*
> *two days later.*

We need a greater desperation and expectation for God to move in our lives. Let's look at one more contributor to teen sexuality.

PEERS AND SOCIAL GROUPS

It's not about what everybody else says to me.
I want to be a virgin because the person I choose to be my
husband will want to be a virgin. It's pretty simple.
—Lizzi, age 14

You could call these social groups a teenager's *circle, squad, posse, clique, team,* or even their *tribe.* Maybe the teen has a *BAE* (someone they value *before anyone else*) or *bestie* who tops their list of importance. Add to these contributors Hollywood, music and entertainment, social media, bad role models, pop culture, failing family and parenting strategies, or an ineffective church. With few exceptions, along with these other cultural influences, most of the sexuality framework in teenagers has come from these peer and social groups.

The blame for a progressive and unbiblical sexuality is certainly shared with all of these. We will talk about most of these things throughout the book, but for now, look no further than a teen's own circle of relationships for another of the greatest contributing factors of teen sexuality.

Often, sexuality formation, thinking, and the resulting behavior arise from the peer group. We will definitely argue in this book that the family is the number one contributing problem to poor sexuality development, but the peer group has been one of the driving forces behind the sexuality ethic in a teen's life. We talk often about peer pressure on young people. But what we *should* be talking about is young people's peer influence upon their friends. It is the responsibility of the home and the church to prepare disciples who are speaking correct biblical principle into their social groups and not the other way around.

You can see there are multiple factors that contribute to a healthy or unhealthy sexuality ethic, including religion, culture, media, the home, campus, sex education, peers, physiological growth, youth ministry involvement, adult mentors, and an early personal theology. These things are not necessarily good or evil in and of themselves. This list could have a positive or negative effect on someone's sexuality development. However, young people must make sure they are choosing the right influences in each of these arenas.

> *All of these factors could lead to a healthy framework for adolescent human sexuality development. These arenas could build a strong self-acceptance, theology, experience, and balance of sexuality education so a young person can determine, without the pressure of negative outside influences, what he or she believes about sexuality.*

Certainly, that kind of maturity takes a while to develop in young people as they progress through the adolescent stage into adulthood. What is clear is that the greater the number of these positive influences, the easier it is for teens to navigate their own personal sexuality ethic.

OVER-SEXUALIZATION

It is no secret that our culture is inundated with sex. Students are reminded 24/7 they are sexual beings. This filter by which they see the world has convinced them *everything* is about sex—the physical world, the spiritual world, their feelings, and their relationships. With this *over-sexualization* comes the inability to compartmentalize sex from everything else.

Let me explain more vividly.

> *From a cultural standpoint, how do we handle an elementary student having a gender crisis or a sexually confusing moment such as being attracted to the same sex?*

From today's *cultural* framework, we know how this is handled. The adolescent is told that it's okay, express yourself, be true to your feelings, and you must be gay. And then, as we have seen recently, we allow our children to choose what they want to be without regard for common sense biblical design, or how this will affect their psychology or identity. That response is normal today and represents our progressive changing culture.

> Temptation usually comes in through a door that has deliberately been left open.
> —Arnold H. Glasow

But sometimes, this issue young people are facing comes from temptation—the scheme or plan of Satan. Satan will often use temptations of any form to get us to succumb to our feelings, our hurt, fear, ignorance, or even bullying. What we do with that temptation or that knock on the door is critical to overcoming the temptations. If we do not handle this satanic scheme with wisdom and power, the door is left open rather than being slammed shut against Satan and his lies!

> *From a scriptural perspective, how do we handle an elementary student having a gender crisis or a sexually confusing moment such as being attracted to the same sex?*

From a *scriptural* framework, let me tell you how I handle this. This happens *several times a month* in my work, and I have had to think this through for many years now. Here are a few principles I use in this situation. Some are simplistic; some are much more complicated and intrinsic.

- If a teenager comes to me struggling with same-gender attraction, my first response is to **listen**. Because they will give me the information I need to process my response. Be careful of fitting everyone into a box or a matrix. People get to their identity in so many ways.

- I **ask questions** as I'm listening to teenagers. Because often they will let you know where these thoughts have come from. Most often, I have found their feelings come from deceptive information from society or peers or their own thinking.

- I assure them that just because they are attracted to the same sex does not mean they are gay. They must be taught to see such things as stealing, lying, self-harm, or sexual attraction as simply a temptation. And **temptation is not an identity.**

- It is important to understand same-sex attraction could simply arrive out of **the setting someone is in**, the circumstances or something that happened to them, the messages they are hearing in music or movies, and the people they are around. I have found that redirecting a teenager from their setting—their past, their music or movies, their friends—has changed their thinking and stopped the attraction.

- It is important to help young people see that environment **is a strong formative system**. All of us have a lean or nurtured tendency toward homosexuality (or a number of personal dispositions) because of our environment or setting. This is normal. Just like some teenagers could have a lean or nurtured tendency toward confidence, education, or swearing, depending on their environment or setting, a teenager could also have a disposition toward homosexuality. But our identity is not our disposition created from an environment.

- I also try to help an adolescent in this situation to understand that **feelings are not necessarily always right** nor should they formulate their personhood from feelings. Teaching an adolescent critical thinking skills is also very important in combating all kinds of teen pressures, such as racism, bullying, or body-shaming. It is a very deceptive thing to say, "I think therefore I am."

- Finally, I show the person it is better to **formulate their identity from an ethic and not an experience.** Natural and spiritual human identity does not come from what someone has said about us, what is popular in culture, from another relationship, or a feeling that we have had. It comes from a scriptural ethic. This is where I take them to the Bible for a theology of sexuality and I help them to see the immediate *deliverance* of Christ from this temptation, or the *discipline* of self that it takes to overcome this temptation.

Listen, I understand that it is much more difficult than this. I know that you may say this is too simplistic. And you are right. But we must move young people beyond becoming products of their environment. Do you see how easy it is to validate our feelings or experiences above an ethic or truth? In the face of an over-sexualized culture that would immediately tell a young person to obey their feelings, we create labels out of experiences and environments rather than ethics. We create labels like *homosexual* or *gay* that become almost inescapable because of the pervasive social deception.

> What would it be like to kiss my girlfriend?
> —A middle school girl

At a youth convention, I once made the statement, *"Same-sex attraction is not sin; same-sex action is."* Afterwards, a young middle school girl came up to me with her youth pastor and his wife and asked me to "say that statement again." I asked her what she meant. And she said, "That statement about attraction!" So I repeated it for her: *"Same-sex attraction is not sin, same-sex action is."* And she began to cry. Then she proceeded to tell me about a recent incident that bothered her.

She had been at a sleepover with her girlfriends. While they were all watching Netflix and lying on the bed, talking, and texting on their phones, she had a thought: *"What would it be like to kiss my girlfriend?"*

She had the thought for days afterward. She struggled with confusion, guilt, and shame—her words, not mine. When she shared her feelings with one of her friends, that girl said she had been having the same thoughts and they must be gay.

But the middle school girl was confused for weeks. Until she walked into the youth convention and heard that one statement.

> *This young lady then realized that just because her **friends** or a **movie** or a **television show** or the **feelings she had in the bed with her girlfriends** or the **culture** says that same-sex attraction means you are gay, she could challenge that argument or that feeling.*

Like anything else in life, simply because we have a tendency or bent toward education, athletics, alcoholism, lying, pornography, stealing, or swearing doesn't mean we are a teacher, an athlete, an alcoholic, a liar, a porn addict, a thief, or a foulmouth. It just means that we might be tempted in an area of weakness and must be *delivered* from this by Christ, and we must *discipline* ourselves from this. If we believe from a scriptural framework that alcoholism, lying, pornography, stealing, cursing, or homosexuality is disobedience to God's created ethic or order, then we must do something with the sinful attractions before they become actions or behavior.

> *You are not a **product** created in the image of pop culture.*
> *You are a **person** created in the image of God. What defines*
> *all of us as humans first are the Scriptures. That scriptural*
> *ethic will always be the design mold for every human being.*
> *Not the culture or our feelings.*

THE NUMBER ONE CONSUMER OF SEX

America has created the hookup phenomenon so prevalent today because of over-sexualization...of everything.

Shallow conversation leads to shallow relationships. We have lost the desire to get to know people and now merely respond to each other externally and not internally. Our relationships have become increasingly surface level and physical as we have forgotten the importance of an emotional and spiritual connection.

We need to talk about *issues* with people and not just the weather. We need to discuss *ideas* with people and not just the current headlines. When is the last time you had a conversation with someone about their dreams and goals in life rather than talking about other people and drama? Shallow conversation will always lead to shallow relationships; deeper conversations will lead to deeper relationships.

Look at what Noel Yeatts, president of World Help, a global anti-human trafficking organization, had to say about America:

> The United States is the number one consumer of sex world-wide, and we've become numb enough to pornography that we're fine with films and TV shows that glamorize this par-ticular issue.... The danger here is that we forget there are people behind this issue, and it causes us to become cold to the sex-trafficking epidemic that is right on our doorstep.

As Christians, we have an incredible opportunity to make a difference.[35]

Let's close the chapter by looking at a very important part of teen sexuality: *dating* and *purity*.

THE DATING RELATIONSHIPS OF TEENAGERS

> *Guys* use the emotional to get the physical— and *girls* use the physical to get the emotional.
> —Jeanne Mayo, veteran youth pastor

The answer to dating behavior begins with theology and not just physiology.

As it relates to dating, the central principle I have shared with teenagers for decades is they do not *need* each other. As much as they think they need another person, we have to help teens understand that their most important relationship on earth is their relationship with God. When that relationship with God is right, every other relationship they have will be right. One of the lessons I learned a long time ago was that two halves don't make a whole in relationships. Two people must bring their whole selves into the relationship to make it whole.

Let's look at two types of dating relationships.

AVERAGE DATING RELATIONSHIP

Boy meets girl. Girl flirts with boy. Boy asks girl to go out. Boy doesn't talk to the girl's parents or guardians. Girl says yes. Boy and girl go

---

35. Leah MarieAnn Klett, "Hollywood is driving global sex trafficking epidemic by glamorizing porn, Christian activist says," *The Christian Post*, August 10, 2019 (www.christianpost.com/news/hollywood-driving-global-sex-trafficking-epidemic-glamorizing-porn.html).

out and make out. Boy and girl go out again and make out. Then boy gets aggressive and girl gives in.

HEALTHY DATING RELATIONSHIP

Boy meets girl. Girl rejects boy. Boy asks again and again and again. Girl decides to go out, but asks him to talk to her parents or guardians first. Boy says no. Then later, boy says okay. Boy meets parents or guardians. They tell boy to pick girl up for church. Boy and girl go to church for a few weeks. Then boy gets aggressive on a date. But girl places her Bible on the front seat next to her. Boy decides he will not cross over Matthew, Mark, Luke, and John to get to her. Disaster thwarted!

Now, I am having a little fun, but you can see the difference in a dating relationship if biblical principles guide the couple.

Over the years, people have bashed dating and given the same concept another name. Maybe it was courting, group relationships, or even the process of engagement. I'm not here to rally against dating. There are principles that, if applied to the practice of dating, can make it an important part of adolescent development.

DATING PRINCIPLES

Here are a few principles teenagers need to have when it comes to dating. I've given them the acrostic *DATING*.

- **Date** God first. Then every other relationship will be fine. Help teens understand the most important relationship to them is Christ. If that relationship is right, then a dating relationship will be right too.

- **Ask** the parents. Teach teenagers to meet the person's parents or guardian, and then to ask for permission to date someone. Talking to the parents or guardian first will bring some accountability to the relationship. Getting to know the parents is like getting to know the child. To be honest, this step may prevent a lot of bad things from happening.

- **Talk.** When you are on a date, never stop talking. Keep talking. Just talk. May there never be silence. Talk. See what I mean? Bad things happen when you stop talking. Plus, talking will help you to get to know each other and know whether you would like to do this again. Are you interested in someone's intellect? Are you interested in their beliefs? Are you interested in the goals they have for their life? Talk!

- **Information must be shared**. Things like return time or curfew, what you are doing, where you are going, and who you are with. Another piece of information you should have is your *list* of what you want in a relationship. If someone doesn't match this list, don't date. This basic information will help your dating immensely.

- **Never be alone**. Never go into each other's bedroom alone, never turn the lights off, never lie under a blanket together, never put the car in park if you are both in it, never go beyond kissing, and never drop her off without going back up to the door.

- **Group dating is critical to development**. It can show teenagers how different people treat each other and how to handle relationships with different types and kinds of people. It also can take the pressure off performing or finding something to do.

I made a list. And if someone doesn't match my list, I don't go out with them. One of the things on my list is that I want to marry a virgin. So that means I'm gonna date a virgin!

—Abby, age 15

THE PURITY AND VIRGINITY OF TEENAGERS

I'm sure you have seen the pro-abstinence T-shirts and merchandise. A popular fashion line boldly declares, "Virginity Rocks."

Recently, a student wore a "Virginity Rocks" sweatshirt to his middle school near St. Louis, Missouri. A teacher removed the student from the classroom and walked him to the principal's office, where the student was told to take off the sweatshirt or wear it inside out. He was also told he could be suspended if he wore it to school again.

What is interesting about this story is that dozens of students have been threatened with the same action from schools around the country for simply wearing the popular shirts.

> *Are we so afraid of offending people that our attempts at political correctness are threatened by a slogan in support of virginity? What does this say about the condition of our society?*

In a statement defending its decision to make the student remove the sweatshirt, Wentzville School District in suburban St. Louis said the shirt was "potentially disruptive to the educational environment," adding, "We routinely have conversations with students around attire that may be inappropriate."[36]

Sometimes, I cannot even wrap my mind around the lack of common sense in our society.

As we have said earlier, Gen Z has shown a more conservative approach to having sex before marriage. However, they have replaced that trend with other behaviors that are sexually explicit. So how can we help teenagers today live a more conservative sexual lifestyle?

---

36. "School threatens suspension for student's 'Virginity Rocks' sweatshirt," *Catholic News Agency*, January 16, 2020 (www.catholicnewsagency.com/news/school-threatens-suspension-for-students-virginity-rocks-sweatshirt-99874).

Obviously, we have given practical principles in this book in several places, but let me offer a few more biblical principles and Scripture I have used to help encourage and strengthen teenagers when they are struggling with their purity.

Look at the strength of the Word to overcome temptation, and the pain of falling into sexual sin:

> *The lips of a seductive woman are oh so sweet, her soft words are oh so smooth. But it won't be long before she's gravel in your mouth, a pain in your gut, **a wound in your heart**.*
>
> (Proverbs 5:3–4)

God's prescription for living holy and pure as a young person:

> *How can a young person live a clean life? By carefully reading the map of your Word. **I'm single-minded in pursuit of you**; don't let me miss the road signs you've posted. I've banked your promises in the vault of my heart so I won't sin myself bankrupt.*
>
> (Psalm 119:9–11)

The apostle Paul's advice for avoiding *aselgeia* or unbridled lust and excess:

> *The night is nearly over, day is almost here. Let us stop doing the things that belong to the dark, and let us take up weapons for fighting in the light. Let us conduct ourselves properly, as people who live in the light of day—no orgies or drunkenness, no immorality or indecency, no fighting or jealousy. But take up the weapons of the Lord Jesus Christ, and **stop paying attention to your sinful nature and satisfying its desires**.*
>
> (Romans 13:12–14 GNT)

Paul's emphasis upon repentance when we have sinned:

*I don't look forward to a second humiliation by God among you, compounded by hot tears over that crowd that keeps sinning over and over in the same old ways, **who refuse to turn away from the pigsty of evil**, sexual disorder, and indecency in which they wallow.*   (2 Corinthians 12:21)

Our crowd has everything to do with our compromise or our self-control:

*You've already put in your time in that God-ignorant way of life, partying night after night, a drunken and profligate life. Now it's time to be done with it for good. Of course, **your old friends don't understand why you don't join in** with the old gang anymore. But you don't have to give an account to them. They're the ones who will be called on the carpet—and before God himself.*   (1 Peter 4:3–5)

These are some great principles to build a teenage life upon. Commit these to memory and you will be able to stand against the temptation in our culture. Remember, the sexual revolution is not going away. Like the proverbial ant holding up its fist in front of the speeding train, the sexual revolution has steamrolled its way into town undeterred. It will take a supernatural response and discipline to stand against the sexual revolution and its temptation.

FINALLY

> My friends are having sex in middle school.
> My friends. But not me.
> —Maddie, age 13

A teenager's greatest win is *not a hookup*, but rather to be able to help solve the greatest problem in their generation. I believe the practical principles in this chapter will help teenagers do just that.

We have to stop thinking that relationships are disposable. That I can just get what I want and then throw it away. We've become numb to the glamorization right at our doorstep. And this has affected how we view a person of the opposite sex. Are they skinny enough, or muscular enough, or popular enough, or rich enough? What can they do *for me*? That is how we look at sexuality and relationships in life now. I know this sounds silly, but *abs* are more important than *absolutes*!

We have lost our absolutes.

> *When one generation loses its absolutes, where will the next generation get theirs?*

When *Teen Vogue* says that *hooking up* can be an ethical choice, then somebody is rewriting the code of ethics. As we have challenged in this book several times, we must base our morality on Scripture, not culture. Our behavioral freedom has rewritten the rules and the codes and we have lost the absolutes that once guided our lives in every facet of living. With the relativity movement, there is no unequivocal behavioral framework for our lives and relationships.

The further we get from the truth found in the biblical values and narratives of *Scripture*, the closer we get to the deception in personal values and narratives from *culture*. This is a simple concept of legacy and heredity, the passing on of mental or physical characteristics from one generation to the next. We have seen civilizations rise or fall based on the success or failure of one generation passing its principles and practices on to subsequent generations.

Asaph, an official who served both King David and King Solomon, wrote about the importance of one generation teaching its principles and stories to the next generation in Psalm 78. It is the responsibility of one generation to pass the *faith*, *works*, *wonders*, *commandments*, *law*, *principles*, *parables*, and the *wondrous signs* of God working in their midst to the next generation of young people who will do even greater things. The story of faith must be told and retold again and again.

Referring to the times when the Israelites turned away from their God, the psalmist wrote:

> Never forget the works of God but keep his commands to the letter.
> Heaven forbid they should be like their parents, bullheaded and
> bad, a fickle and faithless bunch who never stayed true to God.
>
> (Psalm 78:7–8)

It is so critical for a generation of parents and youth leaders to train up their children, teens, and young adults in the faith. The sustainability of the church depends on it. Are we going to see the *church* or *society* set the moral code for this generation? Will we see *youth ministry* or *youth culture* set the moral code for this generation? Is it going to be the *family* or an *icon* that parades the moral code for this generation? I believe the greatest way to win a generation is to help its members reach their own!

My friends are the ones who help me the most. I couldn't stay a virgin without my friends.
—Justice, age 18

Sin, blasphemy, heresy—all these are primitive ideas created by primitive creatures, unworthy of the title "human." These terms have no place in the society of thinking humanity. If any creature advocates for such ideas, then rest assured, it is a mindless ape, not a civilized human. To be called as a human, one has to act like one. In the rapidly disappearing world of these apes, homosexuality falls in the category of sins. Can you imagine, somebody telling you, your love for your dearly beloved is a sin! Can you imagine, somebody telling you, women are inferior to men, and are meant only to serve the men! Can you imagine, somebody telling you, a man can have multiple wives, and yet be deemed civilized! Here that somebody is a fundamentalist ape—a theoretical pest from the stone-age, that somehow managed to survive even amidst all the rise of reasoning and intellect.   —Abhijit Naskar[37]

37. Abhijit Naskar, *Either Civilized or Phobic: A Treatise on Homosexuality* (Neuro Cookies, 2017).

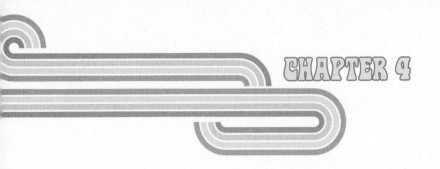

CHAPTER 4

FIVE SOCIAL WAVES

Social Sexuality

Can you imagine someone telling you that driving 70 miles an hour in a 55 mph zone is against the law? Can you imagine someone saying that taking food from a convenience store shelf without paying for it, even though you are homeless, is against the law? Can you imagine someone telling you that placing nude photos on social media platforms is against the law? So what is the problem?

Maybe the problem is that such a person *"somehow managed to survive even amidst all the rise of reasoning and intellect."*

The sexual revolution tsunami has crashed upon the shores of Gen Z, and it has left behind all kinds of debris. *But it does not have the right or the authority to redefine sexuality.*

The Abhijit Naskar quote at the beginning of this chapter is a common belief, if you will, from the progressive crowd toward Christianity. I get Abhijit's statement. If it were true. If somebody were to read his statement and not do any critical thinking, they would pile on and condemn the church for being "primitive" and "mindless." But assuming he is talking about Christianity and the Scriptures here, there is so much bias and untruth with his statement.

37. Abhijit Naskar, *Either Civilized or Phobic: A Treatise on Homosexuality* (Neuro Cookies, 2017).

Bias one, subjective moral reason and intellect are the moral authority over the objective moral absolutes of Scripture. The problem here is reason and intellect are changing, but the objective absolutes in Scripture are constant.

Bias two, when we can be okay with *civil* absolutes like laws, ordinances, and codes, but there is something inherently wrong with *moral* absolutes when it comes to sin.

Bias three, the Scriptures support an inferiority complex toward women and they were *"meant only to serve the men."* A thorough review of Scripture shows the value of women and proves this bias completely erroneous.

Bias four, the Scriptures condone polygamy. This is not accurate. In fact, in the biblical text, polygamy gets no support; it's associated with calamity or disaster or simply exists but without approval.

And finally, *bias five,* the church and Scripture do not allow you to love someone. Understand, there is a difference between loving someone and committing sexual acts or marrying outside of the biblical design. Love is not limited in Scripture, but sexual morality is. God made it clear throughout His Word that marriage is meant to be between one man and one woman, period.

Our culture is filled with all kinds of ideology, reason, and intellect twisting the Scriptures to say what is not meant. This kind of reckless personal ideological thinking enhances the social problem as it wanders further from the morality base of the Bible.

Before we talk about the five social waves, let's hit the demographics of the generational sets—specifically the Millennial and the Gen Z sets.

SOCIAL STATISTICS

Let's look at a quick comparison of the generations, but with a deeper dive into the last two generations that comprise the largest number of people in the U.S., the Millennials and Gen Z. This data is taken from a compilation of demographic research articles from Pew Research Center and the Barna Group.

BABY BOOMERS

Birth years: 1944 to 1964

Current age: 55 to 75

Generation size: 72 million

Media habits: Baby boomers are the biggest consumers of traditional media such as television, radio, magazines, and newspapers. Despite being so traditional, 90 percent of boomers have a Facebook account to stay in touch with family members or reconnect with old friends. Some have adopted technology such as cloud-based voice services and smartwatches.

Shaping events: The optimism of post-World War II, the Cold War, and the hippie/Jesus People movement.

GEN X

Birth years: 1964 to 1979

Current age: 41 to 56

Generation size: 76 million

Other handles: Latchkey Generation, MTV Generation

Media habits: Gen X still reads newspapers and magazines, listens to the radio, and watches TV (about 165 hours' worth per month). Although they spend much less time than their children online and are not quite adept at all social platforms, they are digitally savvy and spend roughly seven hours a week on Facebook and other platforms.

Shaping events: End of the Cold War, the rise of personal computing, and disasters such as the explosion of the space shuttle Challenger, the Three Mile Island meltdown, and the Iranian hostage crisis.

MILLENNIALS

Birth years: 1980 to 1997

Current age: 23 to 40

Generation size: 89 million

Other handles: Gen Y, Gen Me, Gen We, Echo Boomers

Media habits: 95 percent still watch TV, but Netflix edges out traditional cable as their preferred provider. Cord-cutting in favor of streaming services is the popular choice. This generation is extremely comfortable with mobile devices but 32 percent still use a computer for purchases. They typically have multiple social media accounts.

Shaping events: The Great Recession, the technological explosion of the Internet and social media, and the terrorist attacks of September 11, 2001.

GEN Z

Birth years: 1998 to 2013

Current age: 7 to 22

Generation size: 92+ million (roughly 25 percent of the population)

Other handles: iGeneration, Post-Millennials, Homeland Generation

Media habits: The average Gen Z received their first mobile phone around age ten. Many of them grew up playing with their parents' mobile phones or tablets. They have grown up in a hyper-connected world, and the smartphone is their preferred method of communication. On average, they spend four to five hours a day on their mobile device, with nine to ten hours a day spent on all screens, including TV and computers.

Shaping events: Smartphones, social media, never knowing peacetime, the division in government, racial tensions in America, the COVID-19 pandemic, and seeing the financial struggles of their parents, which has made them more financially conservative.

A DEEPER LOOK AT MILLENNIALS AND GEN Z

It is no secret that youth dominate culture in America. And by youth, I mean the Millennial and the Gen Z set.

The Millennials are the demographic set that followed the Generation X of the 1960s through 1980. And they would watch the second millennium change arrive on planet earth in 2000. Millennials are the older brothers and sisters—or perhaps even the parents—of the last demographic to be tagged, Generation Z, the present generation of teenagers. Gen Z, as they would be called by their shorter moniker, are the teenagers and adolescents of today. These two sets are what we have called youth in this book.

Young people in the Millennial and the Gen Z sets are the focus of our society and the popular way of life in modern America. Youth are at the center of the top social and cultural issues of the twenty-first century—racial diversity and inclusion marches, gun violence, human trafficking, global causes like water wells and human trafficking, voting in the presidential election, social media, economics, and the sexual revolution, to name a few. Additionally, they are in the spotlight of every marketing and advertising company.

Youth are constantly being courted by the *merchants of cool*, the creators and marketers of pop culture for teenagers. Gen Z has a spending power of $143 billion.[38] At some point, we must see them for who they are and not for how they can be used. As youth leaders, we must shape this powerful resource God has entrusted to us and value them as people, not as a commodity.

> *Teenagers are a coveted consumer demographic because it's believed they aren't yet brand-loyal, so there's time to sucker them into adopting one. They're also in the sweet spot between "just began working" and "not yet paying off student loans."*

These young people in the Millennial and Gen Z sets are going to define the next era in American life. They will do that as they *redefine* the sexual revolution, *reimagine* the information and artificial intelligence (AI) arenas, *redirect* the social media phenomenon, *recover* the disintegration of the family, and even *reinvent* how to deal with causes such as racial diversity and inclusion, anti-human trafficking, bullying, and humanitarian work.

Young people in America today are writing another chapter in our history. In world history, too, for that matter.

DEMOGRAPHICS

Let's look at some different numbers.

A global picture will prove a large portion of the world population consists of teenagers and young adults. This fact alone underscores the importance of ensuring there is a sustainability plan for the church.

---

38. Joe Cardador et al, "The Power of Gen Z Influence: How the Pivotal Generation is Affecting Market Spend," BarkleyUS, January 2018 (www.millennialmarketing.com/wp-content/uploads/2018/01/ Barkley_WP_GenZMarketSpend_Final.pdf).

The latest Census Bureau statistics (as of February 2019) show the top ten populated countries in the world are:

1. China 1,389,618,778

2. India 1,311,559,204

3. U.S. 331,883,986

4. Indonesia 264,935,824

5. Pakistan 210,797,836

6. Brazil 210,301,591

7. Nigeria 208,679,114

8. Bangladesh.. 161,062,905

9. Russia 141,944,641

10. Mexico... 127,318,112

According to the United Nations Office of the Secretary-General's Envoy on Youth, there are about 1.8 billion youth in the world ages ten to twenty-four.[39] They would make up the largest country in the world today if they lived in one place.

Can you imagine that setting? I would move to that country! This is a significant percentage of the world population. Almost one-third.

Figures from the U.S. Census Bureau show that there are 73 million people in the U.S. under age eighteen and 30 million ages eighteen to twenty-four.[40]

---

39. United Nations report, "Youth 2030: Working with and for Young People" (www.un.org/youthenvoy/wp-content/uploads/2018/09/18-00080_UN-Youth-Strategy_Web.pdf).

40. U.S. Census Bureau, "Annual Estimates of the Resident Population for Selected Age Groups by Sex for the United States: April 1, 2010 to July 1, 2019" (www.census.gov/data/tables/time-series/demo/popest/2010s-national-detail.html).

> *Youth development and youth engagement are cross-cutting*
> *issues in the 2030 Agenda for Sustainable Development and*
> *other internationally agreed frameworks, as well as a central*
> *aspect of U.N. Security Council Resolutions 2250 (2015)*
> *and 2419 (2018). Each of these acknowledges that young*
> *people play an important and positive role in the realization*
> *of sustainable development, in the prevention of crises, and*
> *in the advancement of peace.*[41]

The U.N. has often recognized the positive role of the world's youth. I believe it is time for the church to do so as well.

Do you see the importance of such a generational set? Can you grasp how critical it is to the future of society that we take seriously our responsibility to raise this generation of young people? Don't just take it from me. Check out the federal Interagency Working Group on Youth Programs at youth.gov or the UNESCO Youth Programme at en.unesco.org/youth to check out the numerous initiatives on youth development nationally and globally.

FIVE SOCIAL WAVES

Let's take a look at five social waves crashing on the shores of our society.

1. THE RELIGIOUS REVOLUTION WAVE

> *The first social wave that has crashed on this generation's*
> *shore is the religious tsunami. What is happening in the*
> *religious landscape of this generation may have influenced*
> *the sexual revolution more than any other contributor.*

---

41. United Nations report, "Youth 2030."

The Millennials and Gen Z are demonstratively lacking in the religious realm. Something that requires our immediate attention. One thing that will be evident throughout this book is the almost unbelievable lack of spiritual awareness among young people in America. I believe some of the statistics prove we need an absolute moral box because of this. The clear differences between the Millennial and Gen Z sets is interesting.

Keep some optimistic vibes going on as we look at the following statistics. In some sense, all is not lost.

Although theology is not a positive development in Gen Z, the current generation is seeing a few favorable swings in some areas compared to their older Millennial siblings. Gen Z is less likely to use alcohol or drugs and is less likely to drop out of school. They have rising grades, are team-oriented, and are more economically conservative.

Alexander Jagaciak and Brett Fink write:

> Never knowing the peace and prosperity of the 90s, Z'ers have evolved to become hard-working individuals who are conscientious and cautious about spending their money. Due to the slow-moving economy Gen Z seeks for stability in life. The big savers associate a convenient lifestyle or product experience not with the term adventurous but rather with the terms solid and reliable....Open-mindedness, the pragmatic approach towards their goals and a unique technical expertise are definitely beneficial attributes of Gen Z which other generations can learn from.[42]

Another later development in the Gen Z world is the long-term impact of the COVID-19 pandemic. Family dynamics, priorities, and

---

42. Alexander Jagaciak and Brett Fink, "Shifts from Generation Y to Generation Z," Medium, July 10, 2017 (medium.com/the-future-of-things/shifts-from-generation-y-to-generation-z-43c353730b72).

spiritual life all changed during the government lockdowns. How well the storms were weathered often depended on whether parents and working-age teens still had jobs.

Outside of these issues, take a look at some of these statistics from the World Health Organization (WHO) as it relates to the sexual lives of Gen Z young people in the U.S. and globally:[43]

- Women have an average of four sex partners during their lifetimes; men have an average of seven sex partners.

- The number one cause of death of teenage girls globally is HIV/AIDS.

- Self-harm is the third leading cause of death among young people ages fifteen to nineteen.

- Almost one billion young people ages two to seventeen have experienced physical or sexual violence..

- The WHO's digital health programs with the greatest level of interest are in category seven, "sexual and reproductive health rights."

- Eighty percent of births by teenage mothers are the result of nonmarital relationships compared to about 30 percent forty years ago.

- Of the 750,000 teens who will get pregnant each year, 200,000 will have abortions.

- Even though the overall rate of teens having sex has fallen, look at the increase of high school students who have had sex in each grade: ninth grade, 29 percent; tenth, 40 percent; eleventh, 52 percent; and twelfth, 65 percent.

- 70 percent of high school students and 80 percent of college students have had oral sex.

---

43. WHO's Sexual Health Fact Sheets (www.who.int/health-topics/sexual-health).

- A mere 3 percent of U.S. adults identify as LGBTQ+ but 12 percent of teenagers say their sexuality is something other than heterosexual or straight.

- Less than half of Gen Z (48 percent) believe your gender is your birth sex identification.

Do you see the point?

Look where personal ideology, humanism, and relativism have gotten us just in the last twenty-five years. Our morality changes annually with the latest flag-raising idea from another movement and a new group of followers join along in the march.

> *What is clear about these demographics is that a generation without a moral box isn't working. And I contend **what we really need is a box**—a code, or ceiling, or walls, or a fence. Instead of moral relativity, what about moral absolutes?*

I don't think anyone in our society argues much about speed limits, traffic lights, or street signs, or about paying for services rendered, how we dress in public, and basic respect for someone else's property. Without these laws, there would be chaos on our roads and in our neighborhoods, supermarkets, and malls. What about, as a society, learning to adjust our lives to a set of common principles or codes again? Sure, we then would have to decide who writes that. But maybe some of this is already written for us.

I believe those principles or that code began for every human being as the Old Testament Ten Commandments were given to us by Moses from Jehovah God. To help a society in Israel know how to live with each other and nature. In the New Testament, Jesus gave us another moral code with His Sermon on the Mount. An application of these biblical truths in this generation—outside of their intended cultural, civil, or religious applications—would be exactly what our nation needs. A set of standards. A box.

> *If we do not build a box or framework for sexuality, we will continue to pay an ever-increasing price for getting closer and closer to a **social** sexuality ethic, and further and further from the **scriptural** sexuality ethic. What is that price? Unhealthy homes, poor sexual identity, pornography, illicit relationships, a lack of respect for each other, the rise in human trafficking, and, ultimately, whatever is next on the sexuality horizon.*

These demographics scream for a new social sexual revolution so desperately needed in America. A sexual revolution based upon an unchanging moral ethic this time. What is needed today is a new theological ethic. Without one, where will the next generation be in a decade? If we do not see an unchanging theological framework, where will social sexuality be in another ten years? Take the time to reread chapter two on theology and real love. We need to counter the loveless sexual revolution going on in our young people today.

2. SOCIAL SEXUALITY AND MARRIAGE WAVE

I don't want my perspective or the government's perspective of marriage. I want Jesus's perspective of marriage. He had one.
—Eric Samuel Timm, Christian speaker and artist

> *The second social wave that has crashed on this generation's shore is a marriage redefinition tsunami. When the marriage reform began to happen in America, the sacredness of the longest institution in humanity was lost and it opened the door for many other sexual revolution battles to come.*

Talking about her split with her husband Offset, singer Cardi B said, "We just grew out of love." Ummm...probably not. Maybe you just never grew *into* love.

Marriage has been under attack for decades now, and it is no new thing that basically half of marriages end in divorce; some statistics say a little higher and some a little lower than half. What is clear is that marriage in the traditional sense in America is a mirage.

We've come a long way since September 1993, when the 104th Congress passed into law the Defense of Marriage Act, or DOMA. *Did you get that?* Our federal House and Senate, representing "We the People" of the United States of America, passed a bill declaring that marriage was between a man and a woman. It was signed into law by President Bill Clinton.

For something like that to happen only a little more than twenty-five years ago seems light-years from today. Popular opinion has changed. What happens within social sexuality, or within social anything, is usually populous at first and then quickly considered principle. Until another idea comes along. And that is exactly what happened to DOMA. How the tables have turned!

As the tsunami was growing out at sea, less than twenty years later, America would be on a fast-track of change for the redefinition of marriage. The sanctity of marriage between a man and woman was thrust back into the national debate when former President Barack Obama announced a shift in his view on the issue during a live interview on May 9, 2012.

Obama said, "At a certain point, I've just concluded that—for me personally, it is important for me to go ahead and affirm that—I think same-sex couples should be able to get married."[44]

---

44. "Transcript: Robin Roberts ABC News Interview With President Obama," *ABC News*, May 9, 2012 (abcnews.go.com/Politics/transcript-robin-roberts-abc-news-interview-president-obama/story?id=16316043).

> *Explaining his reasoning for supporting same-sex marriage,*
> *Obama said he thinks not only about "Christ sacrificing*
> *himself on our behalf," but also the golden rule: "Treat*
> *others the way you'd want to be treated.... That's what we*
> *try to impart to our kids.... That's what motivates me as*
> *president.... I figure the more consistent I can be...to those*
> *precepts—the better I'll be as a dad and a husband, and—*
> *hopefully the better I'll be as a president."[45]*

Let's be clear. I'm a fan of Barack Obama as a husband and father. I've spoken many times of my admiration for the way he's raised two wonderful daughters and had such a strong marriage, serving as an encouraging example to our nation.

However, by any standard of exegesis, it was a huge misstep to use Christ's sacrifice and the Golden Rule to defend same-sex marriage. Additionally, Obama said his decision to make a statement was a result of discussions he had with his family, speaking to his political team, and listening to friends on the matter. Aside from my general disagreement with the former president's viewpoint, it is no secret that the Scriptures are being taken out of context to promote a moral stance.

What is so stunning, however, is how widespread one person's statement can influence society and change the law just a short time later. With an emphasis upon the Constitution and without much critical thinking or examination of the Scriptures, by June 2015, DOMA was overturned, and by a 5–4 vote, the Supreme Court ruled that same-sex marriage was legal in America.[46]

Bestiality

Let's look at another proof of eroding and decaying principles over the course of time by reviewing a related thought on social change and

---

45. Ibid.
46. United States Supreme Court opinion *Obergefell v. Hodges* (www.supremecourt. gov/opinions/14pdf/14-556_3204.pdf).

sexuality issues. How much longer do we have to wait for other issues of morality to go through the same change? Is it just a matter of the right people at the right time—or, rather, the wrong people at the wrong time—dismantling another common sense biblical moral absolute?

You can think I'm crazy to bring this up, but I have spoken of this several times in different settings over the past ten years. Today, bestiality is considered an unacceptable sexual practice. I dare say 95 percent of Americans would agree that it's wrong. However, if you were to Google the issue, you would see the shift has already made social conversation, and the narrative is well on its way to becoming an open populist change in our society.

The Berlin-based organization ZETA-VEREIN (Zoophiles Engagement for Tolerance and Enlightenment Society) says:

> We zoophiles do not want to be rubberstamped as sadists, but be seen as real people with a genuine sexual orienta-tion (as e.g. homosexuality is) which incorporates to love an animal as one can love a human. We condemn horse ripping, the killing of dogs and similar at least as much as the next normal person. Another problem we are facing in the struggle for tolerance is that most people recognise animals only as asexual entities, which are not believed to particularly enjoy intercourse in general. Such a stance has been scientifically disproven long ago. We'd therefore want to battle this mis-conception in favour of the idea that it may be possible to be intimate with an animal without hurting it, without the need to specifically train such a performance.[47]

---

47. www.zeta-verein.de/en/the-association.

Other Sexual Practices

A growing number of people are involved in other sexual activities that fall outside the biblical standard set by God. Objectophilia. Necrophilia. Paraphilic infantilism. There are dozens of philias.

We cannot replace a history of public thought and biblical morality on any topic because we have become more politically correct or have wandered from the Scriptures so far as to change basic common sense. When our country starts to make morality decisions based upon peer thought, general consensus, and the misuse of Scripture, we are making a shift away from absolutes. Something I believe will continue us down a spiraling path from which we will not recover. Since when did prevalence or consensus become the basis of our moral decision-making? Especially when it comes to ethical standards.

3. THE GENDER NONCONFORMING WAVE

The third social wave that has crashed on this generation's shore is the gender tsunami. What was once human genome sanctity, gender binary is now pushed aside for a spectrum of choices.

Welcome to the gender revolution happening all around us and growing with every passing year. You can see the upheaval in government legislation, public schools and higher education, the military, and now daily in the legal system. America moved quickly from a binary, male/female gender ethic to a nonbinary spectrum of genders just in the last five years.

If you are not familiar with the following terms, you are behind the gender sexuality movement in 2020 America:

- *Gender spectrum*: a pansexual array of gender choices

- *Gender confirming surgery*: transformation surgery to gender of choice

- *Nontraditional gender roles*: roles falling outside the historical male or female narrative

- *Gender nonconforming*: not confined to expected gender

- *Ambiguous genitalia (intersex)*: born with variable, multiple, or partial genitalia or chromosomes

- *Gender norm transgression*: going beyond expected gender norms

High School Athletics

Take a look at the recent struggle over transgender athletes competing in high school sports. The U.S. Department of Education Office for Civil Rights (OCR) ruled that the Connecticut Interscholastic Athletic Conference (CIAC) and the Glastonbury school district violated the rights of female student athletes by allowing male-to-female transgender athletes to compete on the girls' track team. The OCR attorneys wrote:

> The CIAC, by permitting the participation of certain male student-athletes in girls' interscholastic track in the state of Connecticut, pursuant to the Revised Transgender Participation Policy, denied female student-athletes athletic benefits and opportunities, including advancing to the finals in events, higher level competitions, awards, medals, recognition, and the possibility of greater visibility to colleges and other benefits.[48]

This is a great example of a loss of absolutes when they clash with previous absolutes, such as the 1972 Title IX legislation protecting

---

48. Revised Letters of Impending Enforcement Action (www2.ed.gov/about/offices/list/ocr/docs/investigations/more/01194025-a2.pdf).

people from discrimination based on sex in education programs or activities that receive federal financial assistance.

This societal debate of transgender privileges in single-sex sports is taking place in California, Arizona, Ohio, and New York, just to name a few places where state legislators are stepping in. It has found its way onto campuses across America. Besides sports teams, transgenders are also seeking entry into restrooms and locker rooms historically set aside for cisgenders.

> With the growing societal challenges to classic definitions and thinking toward sexuality have come increased tensions between the church and religious organizations. As far as I am concerned, the church bears much of the blame for not holding fast to a biblical theology of love and sexuality.

The church must be a principled, calming, and affirming voice in this conversation.

Owning the Middle

A person's gender has always been elementary to their existence and identity. It has been sacred. Until now. In the last few years, we have seen a redefinition of gender sexuality. As we stated earlier, maybe some of the depression and suicide we see in our Gen Z set is caused by identity confusion. Despite what we may want, in society, sexuality is now fluid and changing at an alarming pace. Here are a couple of findings related to the societal battle of gender identity:

- Encouraged by psychologists and other "experts," the push for gender-neutral parenting appears to be on the rise. In an interview with *Parents* magazine—found in doctors' offices across the U.S.—one psychologist said, "Our society that is so gendered is not really setting our kids up for success.

Gender-neutral parenting thinks about fostering good skills or traits for all humans to grow up with."[49]

- When government forms are being challenged to include a "third way" or middle ground in sex designation, I think we can safely say that gender identity in America is under review and ultimately redefinition. In one study by the Barna Group, only 48 percent of Gen Z believe sexuality is defined by the birth sex designation. And 33 percent believe sexuality is determined by how a person feels.[50]

With the proliferation of this narrative on television and in the media, music industry, pop culture, and movies, it's no wonder the sexual revolution has been like a tsunami wave crashing over America. Social communication has changed the pace of evolution. This was never more defined than by a 2013 interview that gave a new meaning for sexuality to young teens all over the world.

When interviewed by ESPN, six-foot-eight Women's National Basketball Association star Brittney Griner spoke candidly about schoolgirls tormenting her by groping her flat chest and high school boys taunting her by saying, "Yo, you can untuck now." Griner said she doesn't see herself as a certain "type" anymore. "I used to do the whole baggy, hard-core, I'm-a-boy look. Then I went through a preppy phase. Now I have the athletic, bow-tie look. I found my style."[51]

She got a flower tattoo with a hummingbird "to show my girlie side," she said. "So many people exist between the two ends of the spectrum, but no one wants to admit it. If you're in between, they say something is wrong with you. 'We can fix you.' Well, I don't need fixing."[52]

49. Alana Bracken, "How to Raise a Gender-Neutral Baby," *Parents*, May 27, 2020 (www.parents.com/parenting/should-you-raise-a-gender-neutral-baby).
50. Barna Group, *Gen Z*.
51. Kate Fagan, "Owning The Middle," ESPN, May 29, 2013 (www.espn.com/espn/feature/story/_/id/9316697/owning-middle).
52. Ibid.

This sentiment and moral shift took place right before our eyes. There are many other examples of this, but the point is simple: our culture is trying to get away from clearly defined principles that place us in a definite gender box. Rules and regulations are now seen as binding and oppressive. At least morally. But certainly not civically. I don't believe anyone in the country would want to do away with civil laws such as traffic lights and speed limits.

With all of this discussion in society, the church needs to bring love into the argument...because we have brought a lot of truth there without grace.

The church does not have to leave its truth at the door of relationship. We should have met the sexual revolution and the gender revolution with a love revolution twenty-five years ago. This would have made a huge difference, at least in the relationship between the LGBTQ+ community and the church. Now, we struggle with being haters and not lovers.

Let's look at another issue in the social sexuality discussion.

4. THE SEX EDUCATION REVOLUTION WAVE

> *The fourth social wave that has crashed on this generation's shore is the sex education tsunami. Make no mistake about it: neither the home nor the church provide the standard voice for sexuality in the life of a teenager today.*

I'll include both the school and peers in this new sex education formation. Sex education in the school system has come and gone with both success and failure. Sex education by peers will never lose its influence.

School Systems

Researchers in the school system sex education programs have not focused upon morality as much as they have focused upon whether their programs help young people to change specific behaviors. That would include preventing teen pregnancies, sexually transmitted diseases, and nonconsensual sex if not abstaining. For the most part, sex education programs have lacked a moral base and have often failed miserably because of this.

The Welfare Reform Act signed into law by President Bill Clinton in 1996 set aside $50 million in initial funding for sex education programs that focused exclusively on abstinence.[53] School districts were excited because they could now receive free curriculum and training. The curriculum was designed to encourage students to:

- Delay sex until they were older

- Use condoms and contraception when they did have sex

- Reduce the frequency of students having sex

- Reduce the number of sexual partners

- Stop the spread of sexually transmitted diseases (STDs)

The success or failure of any program rises or falls at the local level, depending on leadership and instruction. The abstinence-only programs were found to be ineffective, showing "little evidence of sustained (long-term) impact on attitudes" toward sex.[54]

Of course. You cannot solve a spiritual problem with natural solutions.

---

53. Robynn Barth, "Sex Education in the Public Schools," *AMA Journal of Ethics*, October 2005 (journalofethics.ama-assn.org/article/sex-education-public-schools/2005-10).
54. Ibid.

The school sex education curriculum was heading in the right direction. However, it did not have the right program content, or, in some cases, the right people, to share the proper principles for the needed change in teenagers' behaviors. There are many good things that came out of that program, but ultimately, it is the responsibility of the home and the church to teach morality.

One of the downfalls was a lack of morality in the material. Wherever possible, the church should be working in tandem with the school system. I have seen this done successfully when a youth ministry professional or a Christian counselor used sex education curriculum from their expertise—and the supernatural result of the training was evident. Sure, we may have to use state-mandated language in the curriculum, but that content is something to begin with!

Sex education programs that include the benefits of abstinence *can* be effective. Researcher Douglas Kirby told the United Nations Department of Economic and Social Affairs:

> Sex education programmes that discuss both the benefits of abstinence and the need to use condoms and contraception to prevent the risks associated with sexual intercourse among adolescents and young people have been effective in changing their behaviour when implemented in school, clinic or community settings and when they involve different groups of young people (that is, males and females; sexually inexperienced and sexually experienced adolescents and youth, and young people at lower and higher risk in disadvantaged and better-off communities).[55]

Government officials will most likely approach sex education programs using different language, with different intentions, but the church should be focused upon some of these same outcomes as well.

---

55. Douglas Kirby, "The Impact of Sex Education on the Sexual Behaviour of Young People" (www.un.org/en/development/desa/population/publications/pdf/expert/2011-12_Kirby_Expert-Paper.pdf).

Peer Sexuality

There's another sex education taking place: peer influence.

Peer sexual formation can be dangerous advice. Especially if a peer group is ill-equipped to deal with the topic. For instance, when a young man comes to his friends and says he's struggling with pornography and needs to quit listening to certain music or watching certain movies, their general response does not hold much authority, partly because they're all listening to the same music and watching the same movies.

Similarly, when a young woman tells a friend that a certain guy has taken advantage of her and she is done with dating, the consoling friend is there...for a while. Later, the friend realizes that young man is now available and she starts dating him. Frustrated, the distraught girl responds by dating someone new.

This is unhealthy peer sex education.

Too often, when peers are left on their own to decide what is right or wrong, bad things happen. Like the example above, immaturity and inexperience can lead to selfish decisions, poor judgment, and even violence or bullying.

Let me tell you about a conversation I had with a young man recently.

This lack of adult leadership in teenagers was never more apparent when I was having a conversation with a young teenager, maybe thirteen or fourteen, while speaking at a camp. He came up to me and wanted to talk, but he wouldn't look me in the eye. He struggled to do so, and I flat out told him, "If you want to talk to me, look me in the eye like a man." That would be a prophetic statement as our conversation began.

Looking directly at me, he said, "I think I'm gay." And then he dropped his head and stared at the floor, unwilling to lift his eyes. I told him again to look me in the eye if he wanted to talk, or I was going to speak with some other students. When he looked up at me,

I could see the shame in his eyes. He told me again, "I think I'm gay. This is just who I am. I can't fight this anymore. God made me this way." And then he gave me a blank stare.

> **"I think I'm gay."** *I've heard this many times. The confusion about what we do, or what we think, or what we have been told turns into who we are. But our personhood is not what we feel like or what outside culture says we are.* **Our personhood is what God has said about us in Scripture.**

I looked him in the eye and stressed to him that he wasn't gay. That he was a young man created in God's image. That no one else could define his personhood. All the while, I was looking at him right in the eye. Face to face. And then I asked him, "Who told you that you were gay?"

As he listened to me, he began to get emotional. So I asked him the question again, and then asked him what was wrong. As he wiped the tears from his eyes, he told me that for five years, people had told him he was gay because of the way he acted. His father, his uncle, and all of his friends. But what shocked me is what he said next.

He told me that I was the first person to tell him that he wasn't gay. I wish you could have seen his face. I will never forget that face. I have seen relief and revelation like this several times as I have talked to teenagers across America and spoken almost the same words to them.

> *Because of the broad progressive departure from biblical truth in our society, adult conversation can set the course of a moral lie in a young person's heart and mind. Or with a broad conservative introduction of biblical truth in our society, adult conversation can reset the course of correct biblical sexuality formation in the life of an adolescent!*

This young man was being told the truth. Not a lie because of a cultural behavior he might have been demonstrating. Or a vibe he was giving. He was completely relieved; he hugged me and thanked me for telling him what nobody else had told him for five years.

He then wrote me a letter I have kept to this day as a reminder of how important proximity is between an adult and a formative teenager. I truly believe that short but direct conversation changed the course of a young man's life.

5. THE GAY/CHRISTIAN HATE WAVE

Here's the final social wave crashing on the shores of our society.

> The fifth social wave that has crashed on this generation's shore is the gay/Christian hate tsunami. Anyone who will truly step back and look at this relationship history can see that the gay community and the church have been separated by untruths, hurt, and anger. From both sides.

The Gay/Straight Hate Debate

Many years ago, a terrible, demonic incident took place that defines this ongoing battle between gays and Christians. The 1998 murder of Matthew Shepard in Wyoming became a global indictment against the church when members of the cultish Westboro Baptist Church picketed Shepard's funeral with signs reading, "God Hates Fags" and "Matt in Hell." Christians everywhere were called haters. His two murderers were called anti-gay haters.

When it came out that one of Shepard's killers had a sexual history with him and some gay protesters turned violent, gays then became tagged as violent people.

All of these labels are wrong.

> *What happened in the years following the murder was a run of legislation, movies, plays, and songs that tagged the crime with homophobic hate and divided the church and Christianity against the gay community. But rather than being a hate crime, the murder was a result of a community without a moral compass, dying in its own ethical setting, that didn't know how to control its own drug-crazed partying, which resulted in disrespect and violence.*[56]

For more than twenty years, the murder trial has been the pivotal moment dividing the church and the gay community.

There's not enough room to walk through this entire incident, but Shepard's killers were not young people who happened to be Christian. They belonged to a small community of young adults in Wyoming who were out of control morally and had no ethical structure. The two convicted murderers also beat several other people that dreadful night who were not gay. Unfortunately, much of the real reason for the murder was shrouded in the clamor that it was a hate crime. The much-needed healing between the church and society has never happened.

At some point, we need leaders on both sides of this conversation to be present and bring healing to our society. When left to ourselves and our own agendas, this is the kind of hateful and violent events that take place.

Another incident took place more recently that demonstrates the divide between the gay community and the church. In 2017, Eugene Peterson, an evangelical pastor, theologian, and popular author, set off a head-spinning pivot on the issue of same-sex marriage and the continuing argument between the two camps. It can be angry and unloving from both sides of the conversation. Unfortunately, both sides went to bed on the first night after the Peterson interview excited

56. Julie Bindel, "The truth behind America's most famous gay-hate murder," *The Guardian*, October 26, 2014 (www.theguardian.com/world/2014/oct/26/the-truth-behind-americas-most-famous-gay-hate-murder-matthew-shepard).

or upset...only to go to sleep the next night with opposite feelings. Because Peterson pivoted on his statement the day after the interview.

As Yonat Shimron of Religion News Service reported:

> In an interview with my colleague Jonathan Merritt, Peterson said he would perform a gay Christian couple's same-sex wedding. A day later, Peterson backtracked, clarifying that he affirms "a biblical view of marriage: one man to one woman. I affirm a biblical view of everything."[57]

You can imagine the cheering on both sides of the argument on two separate evenings. However, this was not a win for gays *or* Christians. It simply defined the problem that has existed between them for too long. And it must be stopped.

I've been in the positive conversations and the negative conversations. We should all prefer to lose the argument and not the friendship. At some point, God is going to work this out in the gay person's life and the Christian's life. Until that time, we must choose to contend for our theology and choose love after the conversation. Even if we cannot choose friendship.

I am asking people on *both* sides of the argument to:

- Value love over being right

- Passionately defend their theology and then choose to love

- Have respectful conversations that build relationships rather than destroy them

- Speak well of each other in their circles and change the narrative in culture

- Place Scripture above culture and history

57. Yonat Shimron, "Eugene Peterson reminds us: The Christian LGBT debate is far from over," Religion News Service, July 14, 2017 (religionnews.com/2017/07/14/eugene-peterson-reminds-us-the-christian-lgbt-debate-is-far-from-over).

- Attend class together, play sports together, have coffee together, and worship together
- Respect our differences and let God work in our lives to reach the world for Christ

It is a difficult balance between love and truth. We know that God has called us to love Him first and our neighbor second. What we must be careful to do is to hold strongly to our theology—and just as strongly to each other. We do not have to shed our truth at the door of relationship. A society that places arguments and beliefs above relationship will never settle anything nor will its people ever have peace with each other or ever be able to reach a society for Christ.

We're going to have to pick ourselves up from these waves crashing over this generation, brush ourselves off, *walk with truth* amid this society, and love *fiercely*.

FINALLY

I know we may never solve the conversation or the chasm between gays and Christians. However, by trying to at least bring about a relationship, apologist Ravi Zacharias lays out a very clear framework for understanding society and sexuality. Here is a quick reference to three ways of thinking Zacharias offers to help process our views on sexuality. As I paraphrase his thoughts on these three influences, you can see how sexuality has changed over the last twenty-five years.

1. THE SOCIOLOGICAL DILEMMA

When you look at the makeup of a society, it becomes clear over time how morality and ethics are formed. Maybe the most formative of those influences is the social framework. This is a pluralistic problem that can be divided into three groups:

- A *theonomous* social framework in culture is one that builds a sexuality ethic from a biblical absolute embedded into the hearts of its people. This framework was similar to the condition of the church when our nation was founded and even as recently as twenty years ago. But that is not happening in America today.

- A *heteronomous* framework dictates the sexuality ethic or absolutes of society from its leadership. It is law or rule coming from outside of one's self. But America is not a dictatorship, so we are not living in a *heteronomous* culture.

- Finally, an *autonomous* framework occurs when a society derives its absolutes and sexuality ethic from personal feelings and experiences. This is probably most like America today.

We are living in an inconsistent and changing cultural milieu with every wind of influence dependent upon any given age, race, background, or geography. We cannot build a society on personal feelings, group think, or pluralism when what is needed is a strong foundation of unchanging and absolute moral ethics. An autonomous framework results in a society that's whimsical and emotional, based upon a shifting foundation of ideas and situational ethics.

> *Can you imagine, for instance, New York City saying that a red traffic signal now means "go" and a green signal means "stop"? That would mean chaos for anyone travelling in from Washington, Boston, or Philadelphia. If absolutes are good enough for civil law, they are even more important for moral law.*

The way laws, legislation, morals, ethics, and codes are created is alarming. Over the past fifteen to twenty years or so, we have seen a major shift in sexuality thought driven by a society drifting from the Scriptures and anchored to personal feelings, thought, and ideology.

This kind of moral situational ethic is destructive to a society. Just keep watch on the bestiality discussion over the next decade to see my point.

2. THE THEOLOGICAL DILEMMA

Protected souls will always lead to protected
sexuality and protected sex.
—Eric Samuel Timm, Christian speaker and artist

We must guard sexuality as a church. Sexuality is the foundation of creation. And a healthy view of sexuality leads to healthy souls. That healthy sexuality is derived from a holistic understanding of what God has given to us in the Scriptures. A biblical construct in our lives is the impetus for our influence on this world. A biblical worldview is hard to find in young people today so we are going to have to rebuild the American Christian teenager in the family and church sectors.

The second framework that Zacharias shares is understanding a sexuality ethic from a biblical and theological framework. What used to be the default in American thinking has taken a backseat to humanistic and progressive thinking in the twenty-first century. The new framers of modern morality view biblical and theological thinking as archaic, mean, judgmental, and out-of-date or old school.

> As the politically correct and progressive humanistic
> thinking has removed itself from absolutes, our morality
> has followed. Once widely held conservative beliefs are now
> old-fashioned simply because society as a whole has left
> traditional biblical truth for populace ideology.

There are many things leading to a loss of theology in culture: the devaluation of the Bible in the family; the church and its struggles with its own emphasis on theology; the seemingly unstoppable surge of humanism and progressive thinking in higher education; the loss of media censorship on the one hand and the loss of media objectivity on the other; and the envelope-pushing conversations in the public sphere. To me, the greatest loss of theology and a significant share of blame must be placed upon the home and the church. Everything else is fallout from the lack of biblical theology in the two places where it's most needed.

The level of biblical decay in America today is unbelievable. This is proven by the diminishing sacredness of theology in the Gen X, Millennial, and Gen Z sets. Over the past forty years, there has been a significant drop in the biblical worldview of each set. The spiral downward began with about 51 percent of baby boomers having a biblical worldview, which dropped to 42 percent in the Gen X set. Things got worse from there. Only 19 percent of Millennials have a biblical worldview. Then along came Gen Z, the "first truly 'post Christian' generation," with only 4 percent adhering to a biblical worldview—the most atheist affiliated generational set in history.[58]

3. THE RELATIONAL DILEMMA

The final dilemma in forming a sexuality ethic in culture is relational. How will a society respond to the diverse forming of moral code? What is the level of relationship and unity between people of different values or codes? Is tolerance consistent?

The relational dilemma is really how we are going to respond to the growing populace movement driven by the moral framework in culture. For instance, the diverse sexuality ethic of people in America results in relational tension between groups and requires open conversations in all kinds of places such as home, school, work, church, and even social media. So what will our response be in the moment of opposition or disagreement?

---

58. Barna Group, *Gen Z*.

> *Tolerance is touted as the new behavior in mainstream*
> *America. But what is so apparent in current sexuality*
> *discussions is a lack of tolerance for the conservative*
> *Christian worldview. Tolerance is the go-to response for*
> *equality until conservative Christian thought is introduced*
> *into the discussion. That inconsistency is definitely not*
> *tolerance.*

Remember that God is a relational God and grants every individual the ultimate freedom of choice. But He does not give us the freedom to change the outcomes of our choices. There is still a moral absolute on sexuality. The social group think or our personal feelings and experience are subordinate to those moral absolutes found in Scripture. At least that is the belief from the Christian worldview.

All truth is God's truth. Let this guide our morality.

When it comes down to the final moral evaluation of sexuality in culture, there must be universally valid sexuality precepts and constructs. Every society has had them prior to the twenty-first century. They were found in consistent exegesis of the Bible—and must be rediscovered again.

When you look at society today, sexuality has moved into virtual reality, digital space, avatars, self-sex, and robot sex. This sophistication of sex for pleasure-only has become a sign of the times. Rather than an expression of a man and a woman in marriage designed by God, the empirical rationale today asks, "What can sex do for me?" Absolute truth has been laid aside for subjective moral reasoning and personal feelings.

It is not possible to love God and hate your brother.
—Russell M. Stendal, missionary and minister

It is important to understand that history, law, biology, and even society serve a theological purpose. If all truth is God's truth, then these serve a theological purpose. Look back at morality hundreds or even thousands of years ago. Morality was served by society; generally, it was unchanging and found in the Bible. But when you look at morality today, it has been served by individual personal freedoms. And it is changing.

When this happens, we end up where we are today. Watching a sexual revolution crashing upon the shores of America like a tsunami. Leaving all kinds of populous and selfish sexual debris in its wake.

Sexuality poorly repressed unsettles families; well repressed, it unsettles the whole world.   —Karl Kraus

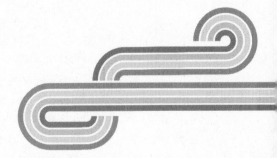

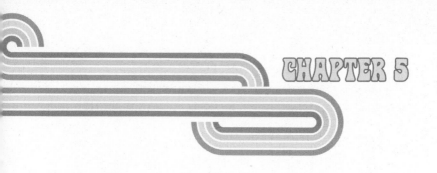

TWO PROBLEMS COLLIDE

Family and Sexuality

In March 2020 during the global COVID-19 coronavirus outbreak, something interesting began to take place in American homes. With the virus spreading throughout the U.S., President Donald Trump issued a quarantine order called "Shelter in Place" to slow its spread. Except for "essential" services, the American people would spend about fourteen weeks sheltered in their homes without being able to go to work (except remotely), attend school or sporting events, gather in public places like churches, theaters, and restaurants, or travel. All public events and gatherings were cancelled or postponed in some form for about seven months.

What began to take place during this order would have a significant impact on American families. Aided by programming and resources from the government, schools, the entertainment industry, and the church, families were forced to be together with no place to go. Like no other time, they would eat together, watch movies in front rooms, play board games, and chronicle it all on social media for the world to see. But what seemed like an inconvenience at first began to yield a change in the make-up of the American home.

> *The research is not in yet. But it will be remarkable to see if we wasted this pandemic or if we purposed it.*

Will the next ten years look different in our society because of this emphasis? Could it be the fruit of a 2020 global pandemic virus outbreak yields healthier homes for decades to come? Will the research prove one of the most difficult times in modern American history puts into motion a family revival? What could be the social impact and subsequent shifts in culture because of the familial relationships that bonded during this time in history? Will identity issues, sexuality trends, academic scores, drug and alcohol use, bullying, theological worldviews, and a multitude of other adolescent trends in children and teens improve?

THE IMPACT OF STRONG FAMILIES ON SOCIETY

This moment in recent American history could have a greater impact on our nation's families than the COVID-19 virus itself ever could. So, how are we making sure we do not waste this moment?

The family is the one institution that exists everywhere globally. There may not be a government, a school, a business, or an entertainment venue in every neighborhood on every continent—but there are families. The family is what shapes every society on earth. For this reason, the family is the greatest evangelism tool the church has ever had. *First*, because the family has the responsibility of raising their children as disciples who will lead in every sector of society. And *second*, because the family lives in the community context, with immediate relational capital and access globally.

I've been praying God would use this moment to turn the family around in America. That all of this time spent together as a family would yield change in so many areas, including sexuality. Seeing our families across this nation spending so much time together is going to impact our nation in a profound way.

> *We may not see it for years, but the 2020 quarantine measures are going to create healthier families and children*

> who will marry and create healthier families and children of
> their own.

This is not a time to be fearful, selfish, or childish. This is a time to be bold as parents, selfless as families, and childlike in our pursuit of God.

> The real question is, does your child trust you enough to involve you in their relationships? Adolescent dating when covered by the wisdom of a spirit-led parent or pastor not only edifies the social maturation of the youth, but also helps develop the spiritual standards that they set for their future spouse.
> —Dylan McKneely, youth pastor

PRACTICAL FAMILY DYNAMICS

Because of the COVID-19 pandemic, I recently saw a teenager post this on Instagram: *"I'm actually liking this time off because we never spend this much time together as a family."* I think a lot of people were feeling that way.

If the family is going to impact our society in a revolutionary way, here are a few practical things that need to take place:

HEALTHY MARRIAGES AND PARENTING

The parents in a home should model honor, respect, communication, and authority. When the marriage and the parenting relationship are healthy, the family will be too. Our children are learning about honor, respect, communication, authority, and identity by watching their parents. A child's concept of respecting their spouse someday will come directly from watching their parents relate to each other. Maybe you are in a traditional home with both biological parents present, or a blended home with one biological parent, or even a home with a single parent. There is no default home in America.

> *I have often watched the best kids come from the worst homes and the worst kids come from the best homes. It is a matter of parental leadership and authority. Build a loving and accepting space that your children will want to run home to!*

THE FAMILY TABLE

What a place of impact! When the family creates a meal together, magic happens. If you could see the impact of the family dinner, you would find no excuses for planning it. I can honestly say my children loved our family dinners—and so did many of their friends! We need to create a discipline and pattern of the family meal at least two or three times a week. The conversations that take place around the table will change your family dynamic.

We always had a rule in our home: you *can* talk with food in your mouth! This is the place where everyone finds out how everyone is doing. It will become difficult for teenagers to hide what is going on in their lives when the family is seated before each other on a regular basis. A family conversation around the table is key to building relationships, identity, and trust.

SIBLING RELATIONSHIPS

One of the dynamics we have lost in our homes over the past twenty-five years are close sibling relationships. I can remember growing up with my brothers and sister and the impact they had on my life. Siblings have a special way of impacting our lives through proximal conversation, accountability, and understanding.

Let's say, for example, that a fifteen-year-old girl is having a difficult time with her boyfriend because he is pressuring her for sex. When the relationship with her eighteen-year-old brother is healthy, his affection and wisdom will keep her from making a wrong decision. As a matter of fact, that boy pressuring the girl doesn't stand a chance when the older brother shows up at his locker to introduce himself! I've watched this play out many times.

Children and sibling relationships must be an important development in every family. Teaching respect and honor among brothers and sisters can bring a huge impact to a neighborhood.

We're not just raising a fatherless generation anymore. That reality is old language. No, today, we are raising a fatherless, motherless, and sibling-less generation. Help our families build healthy relationships with each other by setting up family meetings, having siblings pick each other up from events, and even helping each other with homework.

FAMILY RECREATION

When is the last time you had a family vacation? My children still talk about vacations we took years ago. Every family could use more of the memories, laughter, and education that comes from the family vacation. Family vacations can create all of these things. Maybe you need to get creative and have a staycation in your area that lasts the weekend and doesn't cost that much. Or maybe spend a day together visiting a museum or park, picnicking, or going on a hike or bike ride.

Another creative way to build healthy families is family recreation. The inspiration and relationship that takes place with movie nights, board games, yard games like beanbag toss, volleyball, and badminton, and sidewalk chalk games like hopscotch can happen with very little cost involved. My son, who lives in Los Angeles, takes his three kids to get doughnuts every Saturday morning! Something tells me they will never forget this.

> *Are you seeing the dynamic culture that can be built in the home? This DNA of relationship, trust, and identity that is placed in a child with a healthy home life will safeguard teenagers from catastrophic decisions.*

Let's talk about one more practical family dynamic.

COMMUNITY INVOLVEMENT

One of the characteristic traits of Gen Z is their love for a cause. That might be wells in Africa, stopping human trafficking in India, or supporting anti-bullying campaigns in their local school. Our homes must become places that are causal and missional for our kids. Volunteering in the community is a Christlike practice that can begin in the home.

> *Maybe you go to a local shelter or a food kitchen to serve the homeless. Or maybe you volunteer at a local nonprofit. There are all kinds of ways for a family to be present in the community where they live.*

Our family committed to providing meals at Thanksgiving. We would go to the grocery store and let the kids choose the groceries and then deliver them to a family in need. Another great way to have an impact on the community is to be involved with the activities and events in your area. Sports teams, fine arts programs, or club involvement are easy to attend because our children are involved already. Try getting involved with the local schools and meeting other parents, teachers, coaches, and even your neighbors.

I think all of us could take some time to create new patterns in our homes that will build strong and healthy relationships that can weather the sexual revolution tsunami raging all around us.

REPRESSION KILLS DEVELOPMENT

Reread the quote at the beginning of this chapter. What a profound statement about communication and repression.

In Ephesians chapter 6, Paul clearly placed the responsibility for obedience and honor on the shoulders of children. By keeping this commandment, children *"will live well and have a long life"* (Ephesians 6:3). It may seem like a tall order for most teenagers.

While children are asked to honor and obey their parents, the latter are not off the hook. Paul warns parents, *"Don't exasperate your children by coming down hard on them. Take them by the hand and lead them in the way of the Master"* (Ephesians 6:4). Put another way:

> *Parents, do not treat your children in such a way as to make them angry. Instead, raise them with Christian discipline and instruc-tion.*   (Ephesians 6:4 GNT)

It's a two-way street of responsibility to build healthy homes. And everyone in the family has a responsibility to figure this out together.

Parents are struggling to be parents of Generation Z because as [online] publishers, students now believe they know what's best for them. If they don't know what is best, they want to figure it out on their own.
—Whitney Tellez, youth pastor

Parents must model a protective and instructive consistency with their children. It is also the parents' or guardians' responsibility to keep open lines of communication. When this communication breaks down, the family ceases to be the *first formative influence* upon their children; ultimately, that influence will come from their culture, peers, and countless other sources instead.

Why are we talking about healthy, strong families in a book about love, sexuality, and youth?

If you review my preface, I mentioned that family is *the greatest problem* in the teen world today. Right behind that looms the sexual revolution. We're making a statement in this book that the sexual revolution is this generation's greatest *external* problem. But the greatest *internal* problem teenagers face today is still the home. When the home is healthy, a young person's sexuality ethic will also be healthy. As a matter of fact, if the home is healthy, not only will the children's sexuality ethic be healthy, but also their culture, peers, school, media, and every other influence will be much easier to face.

THE MYTH OF AVOIDANCE

Let me debunk a parental myth. Maybe you have said this before: *"If I avoid it then it will go away."* Hopefully, as parents and leaders, we have learned that is not true. I know if you're a teenager reading this, this is your motto.

But rarely is this ever true. Repression or avoidance kills development. We cannot be afraid to deal with our problems. A healthy home will not allow things to be covered up or repressed because we're afraid to talk about the issues. The opposite is true. The family that can become comfortable with tense conversations will solve more problems than otherwise.

Tough conversations that don't skirt the truth are necessary to child and adolescent development. It is a repressive atmosphere that becomes toxic because our children never get a chance to process their beliefs or talk about their problems with an adult. Avoiding tough conversations will stunt the growth of our children. When our children do not process the information around them with their parents, they will process that information with their peers and others. This keeps them from building a framework for their worldview on all kinds of values development such as morality, ethics, race, religion, and sexuality identity.

> *The family is the first source that must help children and teenagers evaluate all of the cultural inputs from their peers and their world. Critical thinking is best learned in the family.*

When parents and guardians have healthy expression in the home and do not allow for repression of questions or concerns, we build trust in our families to deal with any problem that comes our way. Conversation brings understanding, clarity, safety, accountability, and relationship.

For example, look at this research about the time fathers spend with their children.

About a decade ago, some study reported that fathers spend an average of seven minutes a day talking to their children.[59] Not even an hour a week. What kind of father-child transfer can come out of seven minutes a day? Now, that is the average. But think about how much time you spend with your children and compare it to the average. The statistic simply proves many fathers are not spending *any time* with their children. When we read statistics like this, it is one of the most telling causes for the condition of our nation.

> *Remember, we are not simply raising a fatherless generation anymore. We are raising a fatherless, motherless, and sibling-less generation. We are raising a generation of children who do not know their parents or siblings.*

The more I speak with teens, the more I find they have lost an authoritative family structure to help them process life in a safe

---

59. Clifton Chadwick, "Seven minutes a day: the modern-day excuse for a parent," *The National*, November 14, 2011 (www.thenationalnews.com/lifestyle/comment/seven-minutes-a-day-the-modern-day-excuse-for-a-parent-1.459183).

place. You could include the loss of an entire family system of cousins, aunts, uncles, and grandparents. The family unit has come apart and this is devastating to a teenager's development.

Repression and avoidance are aided by the loss of family structure and relationship.

HUMAN TRAFFICKING

One more result of a repressive family approach can be seen in the worldwide crime of *human trafficking*.

No doubt human trafficking is one of the more tragic outcomes of our dysfunctional family, church, society, and sexuality. To deal with the sexual revolution and not address human trafficking would be irresponsible because it is one of the growing concerns in the youth culture and the world today. It has become a cause of great concern for teenagers and young adults. The human trafficking problem could include child forced labor, minors coerced into crime, organ harvesting, or even child soldiers. But the majority of victims are sexually exploited.

The lure of sex traffickers plays right into the acceptance and relationship vacuum in a teenager's life by appealing to them at their surface level first ("You are so beautiful," or telling a younger target, "You must be eighteen or nineteen") and then at the felt-need level second ("We're like a great big family," or "You could make a lot of money"). Flattering or welcoming a young teenager who is struggling at home or not fitting in with the right crowd is a setup to appeal to them to consider joining this awesome group who will take care of them. That is why it is so important to build healthy conversations and relationships with teens in the youth ministry.

Where there is no expression, we get repression. And repression is a breeding ground for traffickers.

Who do we want teaching sexuality to our children? If the family structure is missing, our kids are going to be taught a sexuality ethic outside of the home. The family should be the safest place to teach children healthy sexual principles. It is the loss of each of these familial relationships that can be fatal to a teenager's sexuality development. Generally speaking, a *father's* authority, a *mother's* love, or even a *sibling's* watchful eye are missing today in the development of the American family.

The impact each of these family roles play on the sexuality and the overall development of our children is lost.

> *Think about it personally. How many times did someone in your family speak into your dating life or even your choice of friendships? I can remember my older sister telling me who I could hang out with and who I could not hang out with. My two brothers and I had a common agreement: we could pick on each other but we would never let someone else pick on one of us. I may have enjoyed bullying my brothers, but no one else was going to do that!*

The role of healthy families creating healthy societies is undeniable.

THE FAMILY AND THE SEXUAL REVOLUTION

How do we change the sexual revolution in a society? I believe it starts with healthy families. A society is changed when the family trains children who grow up and lead in every sector, including government, education, business, entertainment, religious, and home. I believe the key to transforming sexuality in culture is healthy children. History has proven that family is the central system of every culture and reformation can best take place in an intergenerational family setting.

Frederick Douglass, one of the important civil rights leaders of the nineteenth century, was famous for his speeches on ending slavery, allowing freed slaves to choose their own vocations, and the important role of the family in society. He reportedly once told a group of slave-owners, "It is much easier to build strong children than to repair broken men."

In his second autobiography, Douglass wrote:

> The practice of separating children from their mother, and hiring the latter out at distances too great to admit of their meeting, except at long intervals, is a marked feature of the cruelty and barbarity of the slave system. But it is in harmony with the grand aim of slavery, which, always and everywhere, is to reduce man to a level with the brute. It is a successful method of obliterating from the mind and heart of the slave, all just ideas of the sacredness of the family, as an institution.[60]

What is clear today is that we need another reformer and a generation of activists to be raised up in defense of the family. Let's not blame everything *except* the family. Let's hold the family to its rightful responsibility.

10 PRACTICAL SEXUALITY PRINCIPLES FOR THE FAMILY

In the face of the sexual revolution, Supreme Court decisions redefining the family, and other large-scale shifts in sexuality, here are ten ways the family could impact sexuality and bring about a national sexual stability in the coming years:

1. The current national and global focus on the family gives it an advantage of awareness that can open **opportunity for the family to receive resources** from the community and government.

---

60. Frederick Douglass, *My Bondage and My Freedom* (1855).

2. Our families provide the best **contextual** way to speak the language of the communities they live in. When a family teaches healthy sexuality to their children, their children change the narrative in the neighborhood.

3. Family is the one system that all of us come from. It is the **genesis of creation**. This powerful concept brings understanding to a home.

4. The presence of a healthy sexuality in the family could be the **one constant that exists globally in every sector of each community**, including neighborhood community programs, education and schools, corporations and businesses, entertainment and media, and religious and para-church organizations.

5. When a family resides in a community, they have immediate access because of the **adaptation** of that family into the life and culture of the local neighborhood. It takes all kinds of people to reach all kinds of people.

6. Missiology is the study of intention and mission in a certain place. What better way to be **sexually missional** than to use healthy biblical families to reset cultural sexuality?

7. When adults and children build relationships and cross the multigenerational divide in their neighborhood, this creates an **intergenerational movement** that is broad and sustaining over time.

8. It is easier and much cheaper to **build children than to fix men**. The impact of healthy sexuality that families can have upon the juvenile justice and court systems could be positive and long-lasting.

9. **Building healthy biblical sexuality in families** has no cost except the commitment to this kind of development in its children.

10. Early childhood ***development centered on the Bible*** has
    proven to improve educational performance and social
    confidence on many levels.

Why is the concept of family and sexuality so important? Because
Gen Z has placed a low priority on the family, especially as it relates
to the family's influence upon their self-identity and their faith.
Family is ranked consistently in the middle and far from the top of
the influencers upon teens in these two areas of self-identity and
faith development.[61] And this is going to take intentional reclaiming
of marriage and the family in the home and in youth ministry in
order to model healthy homes to a generation who are not seeing it.

The strength of the family can become a force in the sexual
revolution when the family produces children who are equipped to
stand against the tsunami raging around them. The family must be
the place where teenagers find the strength to solve their generation's
greatest problem.

> *Theologian and minister Ray Vander Laan believes we can
> learn a lot from the ancient Jewish education traditions,
> which had children studying and memorizing the Torah
> beginning at age five. At age twelve, boys might be selected
> to continue their studies, and those chosen to become rabbis
> would be schooled up until age thirty.*

The discipleship of children played a major role in the early church. If
a youth did not find a rabbi who accepted him as a student, he would
most likely enter the workforce in his mid-teens. The disciples were
already working at their trades when Jesus chose them to follow
Him. No doubt the life of Christ was draw enough, but each of them
were ready to begin a life of learning under the Master. And because
rabbis were allowed to begin their instruction at age thirty, the fact

---

61. Barna Group, *Gen Z.*

that Jesus began teaching at that age is strong proof that He chose these young men as His first students.

Jesus gave the disciples a family. And that family prepared them to change the world. We need similar families who will prepare our young people in the same manner. There may not be a more formative framework in a teen's life. Whether that is seen in the structure or the emotional support that a family can model, it is the one place that dominates most of a teen's life. At least by the measurement of time.

The loss of healthy family relationships has added to the influence of outside acceptance and coercion in the lives of our youth. I believe healthy families create healthy children. And healthy children will ultimately create a healthy society.

So, what does healthy sexuality in a Christian home look like? What makes a family a liability? What gives a family credibility?

10 SIGNS OF A SEXUALLY HEALTHY HOME

1. Prioritizing the **Bible** as the authoritative moral framework, with the Scriptures guiding family behavior.

2. There is a **balance** of lived experiences between the home, church, school, workplace, and the community. This assures a symbiotic relationship in spiritual, social, and sexual formation between the culture and the Scriptures.

3. The atmosphere is **constructive and affectionate**. Loving and genuine relationships create a safe place to develop strong identities.

4. Parents must model a **healthy sexual relationship** in front of the kids by displaying public affection and speaking words of affirmation so the children learn what marriage should be like.

5. Children are ***respectful of each other*** and honor each other. This internal example will model healthy interpersonal relationships outside the home.

6. Family ***behavior*** at home and in the church, school, workplace, and community are consistent. Worship, prayer, devotion, and spiritual discussions are not reserved for the church setting.

7. ***All members of the family know*** how everyone else is doing. Developing spousal, parental, and sibling communication will increase familial accountability.

8. Parents and children converse with ***forgiveness and grace*** as they build healthy relationships. This allows the family to fail openly and help each other move forward after failure.

9. A ***Sabbath day of rest is vital*** to family sanity and strength. A Sabbath will separate children from unhealthy relationships; plan a day without outside relationships, assignments, chores, social events, or deadlines.

10. Make memories and deepen family relationships with ***vacations***, ***staycations***, or ***day trips***. These can become anticipated renewals that reset the family priorities.

If something like this became the ten commandments of how families operated, can you imagine how different the world would be? The greatest problem in a teenager's world is not the government, education, social media, the corporate world, or an out-of-control media. It's unhealthy family formation. When families are heathy, society will follow.

THE POWER OF THE FAMILY

During the 2015 riots in Baltimore, Maryland, following the death of Freddie Gray, Toya Graham became the "Mother of the Year." Maybe you have seen the video of Graham walking into the middle of the crowd of rioters on the streets of Baltimore and pulling her son out of the fray. With hundreds of protestors on the streets, she found her son and *escorted* him quite physically off the streets, away from the violence and into her waiting parked car. Her actions became one of the iconic moments of the year in the middle of the heartbreaking riots.

While doing hundreds of interviews in the weeks and months to come, Graham was asked why she stepped into such a dangerous scene to grab her son and remove him from the rioting. Her response has been consistent and demonstrates one of the most powerful statements about the family. She said, "That's my only son and at the end of the day, I don't want him to be a Freddie Gray.... I don't want to lose my son to the streets."[62]

FINALLY

Our families are the best place to model healthy marriages so that our children can in turn build healthy marriages and families once they leave the home. The love and sexuality defined in the home is revolutionary to developing children. That's why you have heard it said here and in many other writings of mine that the family is the number one problem and the number one solution in America.

> *We have to stop blaming everyone and everything else for the condition of America and begin to look at the home. Our nation and its problems mimic the health or the unhealthiness of the home.*

Pastor and theologian Dietrich Bonhoeffer was unambiguous about the importance of the family and sexuality. He addressed not only the *gender specificity* of marriage, but also the *sanctity* of marriage between a man and a woman. He wrote:

62. Evan Bleier and Louise Boyle, "My pastor is going to have a fit," *Daily Mail*, April 29, 2015 (www.dailymail.co.uk/news/article-3059827/Toya-Graham-Baltimore-mom-speaks-dragging-son-riot.html).

God is guiding your marriage. Marriage is more than your love for each other. It has a higher dignity and power. For it is God's holy ordinance, by means of which he wills to perpetuate the human race until the end of time. In your love you see your two selves as solitary figures in the world; in marriage you see yourselves as links in the chain of the generations, which God causes to come and go to his glory and calls into his kingdom. In your love you see only the heaven of your bliss, through marriage you are placed at a post of responsibility towards the world and to mankind. Your love is your own private possession; marriage is more than a private affair, it is an estate, an office. As the crown makes the king, and not just his determination to rule, so marriage and not just your love for each other makes you husband and wife in the sight of God and man.[63]

In this last section, I want to give you some ideas for ensuring very practical family dynamics. Use these however you would like in your personal development as a parent or child.

HEALTHY SEXUALITY CONVERSATIONS AT HOME

- Have **regular family dinner and devotions** at least two nights a week and make sure children feel free to speak candidly and ask questions.

- Start your **faith conversations and sexuality discussions early** because your children are having these conversations earlier than ever before. You can decide how much to share with your children and their ability to understand.

- Prepare your children ahead of time by telling them when **family time** will be scheduled each week and tell them what you are going to be talking about weekly.

---

63. Dietrich Bonhoeffer, *Letters and Papers from Prison* (New York: Macmillan Company, 1953).

- No **topic is off limits** at home because that is the best place for your children to hear the truth.

- If you need to have a corrective discussion, have it in a **controlled environment** and not just in an emotional argument when something goes wrong.

- Make sure you let your children **ask questions**. This will help you to know what they are thinking. Here are three easy questions you can start with: first, find out who your children are hanging out with; then you can scope them out on social media and talk with their parents when you see them in the community. Second, ask your children what is going well with their life and what is not going so well. Third, ask them for a weekly update about grades, sports teams, and other outside activities, such as work.

- If you are not sure how to do this, **speak with other parents** who have done this successfully.

- The most important element in family conversations is **clearly** and **early**!

SOME TOPICS PARENTS SHOULD BE TALKING ABOUT WITH THEIR CHILDREN

- **Goals**: Ask them about their dreams, visions, and goals for their life

- **Identity**: Spiritual and sexual identity from a biblical and cultural perspective

- **Theology**: Look at the theology section of this book for key sexuality Scriptures

- **Language**: What is the current terminology in the sexuality discussion? The trends?

- **Behavior**: Among other things, sexual respect for self and for others

- **Media**: Develop an *end user agreement* for movies, music, gaming, and social media

- **Dating**: Every family should have clearly defined and early, agreed-upon dating guidelines. Here are a few: the type of person teens are allowed to date, at what age, curfews, amount of time spent together weekly, location for dates, and creative activities for dating. Our children must also understand parameters for affection in their dating relationships.

> It is critical that you start this early so your children know they can talk to you about anything. This ideal will create early sexual formation in adolescents. In some cases, you can also suggest that your children can talk to another adult whom they trust. This was important to me when my kids were growing up. In the same way, as a youth pastor, I filled that role for many parents.

The cornerstone of society is the family, and the central problem in society is the sexual revolution. These two great forces must work together to solve the greatest of a generation's problems! None of us have a perfect family. But the future of every nation and society is built upon the foundation of its families.

The family is preparing future politicians, clergy, educators, business entrepreneurs, entertainers, mothers and fathers, doctors, and lawyers. Our nation will inherit the most valuable resource the family can give to it: our children.

> I believe the answer to all of society's problems is found in healthy biblical families. Why? Because, as Frederick Douglass said so eloquently, it is easier to **build strong children** than it is to **repair** broken men and women.

SCRIPTURES TO SUPPORT FAMILY THEOLOGY

Honor your father and mother so that you'll live a long time in the land that God, your God, is giving you.   (Exodus 20:12)

Start with GOD—the first step in learning is bowing down to GOD; only fools thumb their noses at such wisdom and learning. Pay close attention, friend, to what your father tells you; never forget what you learned at your mother's knee. Wear their counsel like flowers in your hair, like rings on your fingers.   (Proverbs 1:7–9)

Intelligent children make their parents proud; lazy students embarrass their parents.   (Proverbs 15:20)

Wives, understand and support your husbands in ways that show your support for Christ. The husband provides leadership to his wife the way Christ does to his church, not by domineering but by cherishing. So just as the church submits to Christ as he exercises such leadership, wives should likewise submit to their husbands. Husbands, go all out in your love for your wives, exactly as Christ did for the church—a love marked by giving, not getting. Christ's love makes the church whole. His words evoke her beauty. Everything he does and says is designed to bring the best out of her, dressing her in dazzling white silk, radiant with holiness. And that is how husbands ought to love their wives. They're really doing themselves a favor—since they're already "one" in marriage.
                                                        (Ephesians 5:22–28)

Children, do what your parents tell you. This is only right. "Honor your father and mother" is the first commandment that has a promise attached to it, namely, "so you will live well and have a long life."   (Ephesians 6:1–3)

It is the task of youth not to reshape the church, but rather to listen to the word of God; it is the task of the church not to capture the youth, but to teach and proclaim the word of God. Our question is not: What is youth and what rights does it have, but rather: What is the church-community and what is the place of youth within it? The church-community includes those on earth whom God's dominion has torn away from the dominion of death and evil, those who hear the word concerning the establishment of God's dominion among human beings in Jesus Christ and who obediently assemble around this word in faith.

—Dietrich Bonhoeffer

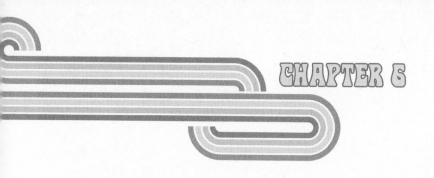

CROWNING KINGS AND QUEENS
Youth Leadership and Sexuality

When I visited Germany recently, I was able to spend some time with the pastor of Zionskirche Church, where Dietrich Bonhoeffer served as the youth leader. On one afternoon, I went to the Bonhoeffer-House, spoke with a tour guide, and heard some personal history of Bonhoeffer and his work. Walking into the upstairs bedroom of the house and sitting at the desk where he wrote *Cost of Discipleship* was surreal.

I love the quote at the beginning of this chapter. You may think it goes against everything youth leadership is trying to accomplish. As youth leaders, we often say things like, "Youth are the future of the church" and "Youth are the most important part of the church." This kind of treatment actually plays right into some of the characteristic traits of the Millennial and Gen Z set. Specialness and uniqueness are part of their DNA. I understand Bonhoeffer's theses and agree for the most part. However, I think you can have both an emphasis upon youth ministry and an emphasis upon youth involved in the church. In fact, many have done this for years.

> *Youth must be placed at the center of the church, not segregated so they hear other sermons and services. The church has separated young people from the congregation*

> as a whole and lost the intergenerational value of their
> development. We must make intergenerational ministry
> an important discipline that will help youth integrate into
> the whole church, not a subgroup of the church. If they are
> separated from the whole church, it will be easier for them to
> leave once they are done with youth ministry—because they
> have no connection to the church's whole life and mission!

Andrew Root, an author and a professor of youth ministry at Luther Seminary in St. Paul, Minnesota, shares his thoughts on the focus of youth ministry in the church:

> We only fortify the generation gap, pushing young people
> off into youth ministry programs and away from the center
> of the congregation. Making young people "special" divides
> them from their parents and other adults, for only those with
> special knowledge can teach them the faith, or even relate to
> them at all.[64]

There is a fine balance between being youth-specific and youth-inclusive.

Really, youth ministry is understanding the totality of discipleship. Bonhoeffer was simply saying we must place *Christ* as the future and the *center* of the church, not youth ministry. In fact, the youth ministry that connects their students with the church will see greater success than a youth ministry that simply subgroups teenagers.

With all of this in mind, let's talk about a youth ministry response to the sexual revolution.

---

64. Andrew Root, *Bonhoeffer as Youth Worker: A Theological Vision for Discipleship and Life Together* (Grand Rapids, MI: Baker Academic, 2014).

INTERGENERATIONAL VS. MULTIGENERATIONAL

Think about it. Multigenerational youth ministry merely suggests the presence of more than one generation, whereas intergenerational youth ministry suggests a relationship between multiple generations. There is great value in intergenerational youth ministry. This kind of ministry will surround adolescents with adults, not simply with their peers. Relating that to sexuality is a huge win because now teenagers see adults with a more developed mindset toward sexuality. Intergenerational youth ministry is a critical part of the sexual development of teenagers.

THE SYMBIOTIC RELATIONSHIP OF YOUTH LEADERS, THE CHURCH, AND THE FAMILY

Youth ministry, the church, and the family are not on the same page. I know this is a sweeping statement to make—and it's not an easy thing for me to say. But it reveals one of the biggest problems that must be solved when it comes to sexuality.

Depending upon your setting and commitment to discipleship, you may or may not agree with my generalization. But hear me. For all of the great things I see in my travels, we are missing an important element in youth ministry, the church, and the family. What we need is greater movement toward a symbiotic relationship among them.

Stay with me. I have the advantage—or the disadvantage, depending on how you look at it—of being in a different church setting across our nation every week. This is an education in itself. Every week, I see a small, medium, or large church, an urban, suburban, or rural church.

> *We have missed two decades of critical theological development in the Millennial and the Gen Z sets because of the loss of the youth leader, the church, and the family teamwork in elementary and teenage sexuality development.*

The youth ministry, the church, and the family must have a more collaborative relationship. The American family has mostly neglected the theological training of its children, while the church has struggled with an oversimplification of theology and youth ministry has failed to see its value, period. What has suffered because of this lack of mission in youth ministry, the church, and the family is a proper theology of sexuality and identity in teenagers.

See the problem like this: *parents* have blamed youth ministry for the problems in their kids. The *church* has blamed parents for not being committed to the church's programs. And *youth ministry* has blamed the church for not supporting it completely. It's no wonder that in the last twenty-five years, families have been disintegrated, the church has lost its voice, and youth ministry has failed to raise disciples. If these three important players in a teenager's life are not on the same page, we have abdicated our responsibility of raising our children to society. As a result, Christians have lost their most important resource and voice in culture: our children.

STRUGGLE ON THREE FRONTS

All three have struggled with their role in sexuality education development.

Youth Leaders

Two things have happened in the youth ministry setting. *First*, youth leaders would like to have a discussion about sexuality but are afraid the pastor or the parents do not want them to talk about certain things. *Second*, some youth leaders are too young and inexperienced to understand how to handle this message with authority.

The youth ministry should be prepared to help the church and the family navigate sexuality. Maybe by planning sermon series and topics collaboratively with a few key families, or simply in counseling with parents and teens. Either way, the youth ministry is often the most capable of dealing with sex education because youth leaders are in the lives of the students.

The Church

Most church leaders have not had a sexuality discussion in their own home, so they have been afraid to have this sexuality discussion with the congregation. Those who have had the discussion at home have filled the calendar with many other priorities, so they may feel like it is the responsibility of each individual family, and they avoid it. For example, when is the last time your church did a full series on sex? Or on theology in the home?

The church has too long been silent on sexuality. Sure, the church has had the right answers. But to the wrong questions. What good is it to have all of the right answers to the questions that no one is asking? I'm sure you would agree, our culture has a lot of sexuality questions. If the church doesn't have these answers, it will be left out of the loop.

The Family

There are multiple reasons the sexuality discussion is not happening at home. It could be that parents lack the confidence or knowledge about how to have the discussion with the kids. It could be a blended home situation and a parent isn't comfortable with their relationship with the kids. And in some homes, there is no desire at all to parent, and the kids are left basically on their own.

Everyone understands the home is where this should be taking place. But for many reasons, we can see it is not being done. It is critical for parents to be honest with the youth leader and the pastor and let them know where they would like help. It is not a failure but a win to ask for help if you are a parent struggling with this responsibility.

At some point, there needs to be a discussion between all three of these entities.

> *The youth leader can approach the pastor and key parents of students in the youth ministry to find out what role they expect the youth ministry to play in sex education. The pastor can have discussions with the youth leader and the parents to assure each that there will be an annual series and weekend of training for the whole church on sex education. And finally, the family needs to find its role in the sexuality development of its children. If this is lacking, the family must have a conversation with the church to ask for help.*

This is where communication is critical. In relationship with the family, the church can be a helpful resource for sexuality discussions.

PRACTICAL SEXUALITY MODELING

Here are a few things every church should do to advance a beautiful sexual revolution in their church, in the families of the church, in the youth ministry, and ultimately upon society:

- Modeling *personal healthy staff family sexuality* in the marriage and with the children; the staff family relationships are a model to the whole church on how to treat each other as spouses, parents, and children

- *Staff diversity* and shared platform for male and female leaders

- *Sermon series and topics annually* that address sexuality; this would include a biblical and cultural understanding of sexuality, clearly defining practices that help protect our principles, addressing the current trends in the sexual revolution, and family dynamics and roles

- Youth leaders must have an *annual parents' meeting* as well as frequent one-on-one discussions with parents

- *Annual sexuality seminar* for parents and children with a guest professional

- *Marriage weekends* to equip parents

- *Graded programming for children, youth, and young adults* that is relevant to their world; assign each department leader to annually collaborate with parents on programming

- Make *family and sexuality counseling* available at the church or through a trusted recommended professional counselor free of charge

These kinds of commitments will strengthen the symbiotic relationship of youth leaders, the church, and the family.

THE PHONE IN THEIR HAND

Teenagers are holding the portal to their future in their hand!

The phone in their hand could drive them away from God. In their hand could be the worst conversations of their life. In their hand, as they scroll through every icon, every filtered pose, could be their worst comparisons and body-shaming images. In their hand could be the most embarrassing moment of their life. In their hand, at the push of a button or the swipe of a screen, could be their next addiction.

Or...

The phone in their hand could drive them close to God. In their hand might be the greatest prayer tool in the history of mankind. In their hand could be the greatest evangelism tool the world has ever seen. In their hand could be the most important spiritual formation tool of their lives. In their hand, with the push of a button or the swipe of a screen, they could have one of the greatest worship tools of their generation.

Am I overstating this? I don't think so.

"Why should my daughter have social media?"

Recently I was with a youth group at lunch, and we were sharing from each other's Instagram and talking about how to use our social media for God. I noticed one of the students did not have social media. Her mother was also sitting at the table. It could have been awkward. But it led to a great conversation. While we talked about the *negative pressures*, *comparisons*, *bullying*, *sexting*, and all kinds of other uses of social media, we also talked about its benefits. So, breaking in, right in front of her friends, the student asked her mother if she could sign up for Instagram. The conversation didn't start very well.

> As I listened quietly, the mother suddenly looked at me and asked, *"Why should my daughter have social media?"* I smiled and walked into the conversation carefully.

I suggested the following: let her daughter sign up for Instagram, and I would be her first follower. Then, every Friday, she would have to use her platform for God. We talked about how to do that, and the whole table was locked in. My guess was not all of the students were doing this. After a few minutes of me talking, all of the sudden, the mother agreed and told her daughter she could sign up for Instagram right there at the table. To be honest, I am not sure if that was a win or not!

While she was signing up, I went over the rules: every Friday, she would redeem her platform by posting spiritual content. And I would be her first follower. Right there, a whole table of students was learning so much about family and much more about social media and sexuality.

That conversation showed all of those students a healthy use of their social media. I'm not too pietistic or too simplistic to think everything is going to be different now with all of those students. But our conversation about content, appropriate photos, who to follow, how much information to include in your profile, and the filtered unreality of images certainly made a lasting impression on those teenagers and their sexuality. I could see it on their faces. Most of them had never had this conversation.

TURNING PRINCES AND PRINCESSES INTO KINGS AND QUEENS

I'm too mature for boys right now.
But someday I won't be. <Wink>
—Rachel, age 15

Sometimes students can make you ride high on the winds of success...and other times, that ride is like a tornado of destruction as everything comes crashing down. It's the nature of parenting or leading young people. Don't you remember yourself at that age? Or have you tried to forget?

When it comes to youth leadership, I have always seen our job description as *"Turning Princes and Princesses into Kings and Queens."* God has given us the responsibility of taking His children from royalty to reign. By creation, every teenager is already a son or daughter of God, even if they are not born again. That makes them princes and princesses. Yet our work isn't to merely leave them at royalty by creation or salvation. We must prepare them to actually know how to serve and reign as kings and queens someday.

Youth leadership must transform teenagers from an adolescent relationship with God to an adult relationship with God, from an elementary and immature relationship with God to a graduate level relationship with God. This may look like helping princes and princesses understand the ways of the kingdom, to help them know how to carry themselves, to help them understand their importance in the kingdom, and to make sure they are ready to hold the scepter and wear the crown someday.

Of course, what I am talking about is discipleship.

> *I see this transformation as a rite of passage. The coming of age. Even princes and princesses have to go through royalty training.*

We have looked at this in the preface to lay the foundation for the book, but one of the iconic passages of Scripture in the Bible is found in First Corinthians chapter 13. Paul is addressing the people of Corinth on their love of gifts and talents. After all, Corinth was quite a city and had a reputation for being spectacular in setting, with gifted, talented people. At the beginning of his letter, Paul even told them, *"You've got it all!"* (1 Corinthians 1:7). In many ways America is much like Corinth.

Paul is dealing with love, the characteristic trait of our faith as Christians. After listing all kinds of spectacular gifts in the first part of chapter 13, Paul says that if we do not have love, it profits us nothing.

> *I may be able to speak the languages of human beings and even of angels, but if I have no love, my speech is no more than a noisy gong or a clanging bell.*   (1 Corinthians 13:1 GNT)

He goes on to describe love in the middle part of the chapter with a fantastic display of love in colorful language. Then he talks about a rite of passage or a coming of age:

When I was a child, my speech, feelings, and thinking were all those of a child; now that I am an adult, I have no more use for childish ways. (1 Corinthians 13:11 GNT)

Wow. At some point in our life, we have to recognize that our growth in Christianity and discipleship is not about speaking in tongues, prophecy, understanding mysteries and knowledge, or having faith to do miracles, or even helping the poor. Our growth in Christianity and discipleship is about love. Everything else is secondary and supplemental; love is primary.

A LOVE REVOLUTION

Given this moment in the twenty-first century, how do we raise a multitude of youth who can bring about *a love revolution* into the middle of *the sexual revolution*?

Here are ten mindsets or approaches youth leaders must have to raise princes and princesses to become kings and queens. To prepare them to lead *a love revolution* that will rise above *the sexual revolution* going on in our society today, and to wash away all of the debris left on the shores of our nation.

1. A THEOLOGICAL MINDSET

We need a theological approach of truth and love toward the sexual revolution. *Our first response must be truth.* In the face of a humanistic and sensual society, we must be salt and light. *Our second response must be love.* Not one or the other, but both. In tandem, *truth* and *love* is a powerful duo of *holiness* and *grace*. This is the pattern of Jesus.

Given all of the changes going on in culture, what is the response of youth leadership to this cultural shift? We cannot meet a shifting immoral society with a shifting theological framework. *We must teach teenagers to be strong in truth*—and meet a shifting immoral society with an unshifting theological framework. *And we must teach teenagers to be strong in love*—and look the world in the eye and not blink in the face of shameless progressive and unbiblical morality. As in every response to culture, we need both truth and love. Although strong love is not always the cure-all, I've seen emphatic bold truth change someone on the spot.

> I struggled with same-sex attraction for a long time. And what to believe. Until a man looked me in the eye and told me, "You're not gay!" That changed my life.
> —Tim, age 19

Modeling a Christian worldview in a post-Christian world is not easy. It will be seen as judgmental and hypocritical. It will be seen as a "holier than thou" approach. But it is not time for the church to waver in either truth or love. The best way to counter this sexual revolution tsunami is to live as Christian as we can in society. Without apology. And with complete *truth* and *love*, *holiness* and *grace*.

2. A CONTEXTUAL MINDSET

Relationship is the avenue to give Christ's love to someone. I believe it is important for every believer to have a friendship circle with unbelievers. Don't confuse this with being yoked or bound in fellowship or brotherhood. As Paul said, *"Don't become partners with those who reject God"* (2 Corinthians 6:14). This is the context of the gospel.

You know the age-old argument. Some leaders live in the *content is king* world, always something to say but no one to say it to. On the other hand, some leaders live in the *context is king* world, where there's always a crowd but nothing to say to them.

This is, of course, an oversimplification of the two.

I believe, ultimately, that *content* and *context* can both reign; the marriage of the two is when effective ministry is accomplished. When both content and context are working together, the church is at its best. It is in this marriage where our approach to the message and the people yields the greatest fruits. The church must take its message into the masses and not expect the masses to make the long and difficult journey to the message.

> *The church's response to the shame in our world will set the tone for the world's response to the grace in the church. We cannot blush or flinch or gasp. But we must look this world in the eye and love them. No matter their behavior or their belief system. We must look this world in the eye and tell them the truth.*

Looking at the world of teens today, you can imagine the kind of conversations that are taking place regularly between teens and leaders. Teenagers are growing up in a crazy and wild world.

- Seventy-seven percent of students experience physical, mental, or verbal abuse in high school.

- Suicide is the third leading cause of death for people between the ages of fifteen and twenty-four.

- One in three girls is abused by a boyfriend.

- One in every 200 teens is harming themselves (cutting, burning, scratching, etc.).

- Almost 16 million students live in a home where a parent is physically abused.

- Gen Z has the largest number of atheists in the history of America.

Some Key Questions

When it comes to relationship with the teenage culture, most importantly, youth leaders must commit themselves to diligently studying our theology and our sociology. Proximity will give us authority in youths' lives. Ask yourself these important questions:

1. *Do you know your students?* Find out about their hobbies, school situation, jobs, sports team, or the family situation. Understand what's going on in their personal lives.

2. *Do you know their world?* Get up-to-date on their music, movies, language, causes that are important to them, and social media. Understand what's going on in their culture.

3. *Are you current in the field?* Speak to other youth leaders. Find out what is common or what others might be doing in youth ministry right now.

4. *Do you listen to students and hear how they feel or think about something?* Instead of doing more talking as youth leaders, let students talk.

5. *When is the last time you told your students you love them?* Not a passing statement, but deep, heartfelt declaration. A youth leader's unconditional love can guard students from committing sexual sin.

3. A TERMINOLOGY MINDSET

Our students are living in an ever-changing world when it comes to sexuality. They know the terms, language, and the latest on sexuality weekly. With everything changing, youth leaders must stay current and be able to guide students through the mess.

Here are a few things you can do to stay up-to-date:

- Follow students on social media and watch what is happening.

- Take one day a month to listen to pop music to help you understand where your students' language is coming from.

- Read and watch the Internet Movie Database (IMDb.com) shorts on movies and series that teenagers are watching. This is a great site to follow pop trends.

- Follow Barna Group, ThoughtCo, *Teen Vogue*, Pew Research Center, the American Medical Association's *Journal of Ethics*, TED.com, *The Youth Culture Report*, and other avenues to stay current on culture.

Every teenager should have a basic understanding of the *nonbinary* and *binary* views of sexuality.

The *nonbinary view* of sexuality prevalent today is a mathematical term meaning more than two. As it relates to sexuality, it is a cultural viewpoint that adds a *third way* or many evolving or transitional viewpoints of male or female sexuality. It allows for and introduces other options instead of what is considered default and binding.

The *binary view* of sexuality means there are only two options. It is the scriptural viewpoint of male and female sexuality, derived from the Bible to define a designed and purposed sexuality from creation.

We have to be able to understand and speak the language of the day.

4. AN EQUALITY MINDSET

Humanity must be valued. Especially living in such a specialized society that places importance on their own kind or type. We must stop compartmentalizing value and see that *everyone* is created in the image of God.

Our teenagers are growing up in a conditional society. Everyone and everything loves them conditionally. If we can teach our princes and princesses how to love everyone equally and unconditionally, it will set them apart in their conditional world. Author Bob Goff put it succinctly: "Love your neighbor, even the ones you don't understand." What a spectacular goal to strive for in youth ministry.

James was the brother (or cousin) of Jesus. I cannot help but think he was probably treated with prejudice quite a bit. Can you imagine Jesus and James walking down the streets of Jerusalem? The crowd is always talking about Jesus, always going up and talking to Jesus, always asking James where Jesus is. That would be a bummer. I think for many reasons James felt a lot of partiality!

> In the second chapter of the New Testament book that bears his name, James said very strongly that partiality is a sin. "If you treat people according to their outward appearance, you are guilty of sin" (James 2:9 GNT). Partiality is when we judge someone and place them in a position of less importance than anyone else because of their economic, racial, or gender status. That is a sin.

Love everybody always.

Our relationship to unbelievers or with believers who may think differently than us must never become broken or tense because of prejudice or judgment. Yes, there is a point in the church setting that requires correction of relationships when we are in fellowship together. But the relationship we have with unbelievers must be kept sacred by both truth and love.

5. A CAUSAL MINDSET

One of the Gen Z characteristic traits is that they are moved by causes. Whether it be bullying in their local school, water wells in Africa, or human trafficking globally, teenagers want to count and make a difference in their world.

Over the years, I have placed a great emphasis on telling students they can do anything. It's that dream stage. Moments are frozen in time as I've watched a teenager realize their life calling or life purpose. I've told them often in that moment that the two greatest days of your life are the day you were born...and the day you realize why. But to see it in their eyes is like watching a flash of lightening!

> *Teenagers light up when it comes to a cause or a passion. It might be education and grades, entrepreneurship and finances, competition and sports, or ministry and calling. As a youth leader, some of my greatest joys have been watching students find themselves in God's plan for their life. It's like an explosion or a big aha moment when a teenager realizes why they were born.*

A dream doesn't have to be big to be important. I'm sure you have heard of the "stadium dream" before. I cannot tell you how many times I've heard students talk about such a dream. I had a student come to me once, embarrassed to tell me about what God had put on her heart. So I asked her to try me. She began to tell me about her dream to fill a stadium full of fans. As soon as she started telling me, I told her I had the same dream. Her face lit up in that moment. *Youth leaders cannot be dream killers.*

When a student finds their cause, they become unstoppable.

6. A FAMILY MINDSET

Have you seen the signs out in front of churches as cars are driving onto the campus? You'll see young and old holding welcome signs with all kinds of creative sayings. Here are a few of mine:

- *We saved a seat for you*

- *Sunday Funday*

- *What a way to start the week*

- *You asked for a sign*

- *You belong here*

- *Welcome home*

Throughout Scripture, the church is described with family imagery. This plays right into the Gen Z set and their team-oriented, family-friendly desires. A family setting becomes the first line of defense against dysfunctional sexuality, illicit relationships, pornography, and unhealthy homes. When it comes to appealing to teenagers, one of the most attractive characteristics of the church should be the family atmosphere. Healthy conversation, plenty of hugs and smiles, an energetic setting, student leaders running around, pre-event activities, exciting music, and a message of belonging can all set the tone for a great youth ministry.

I have watched students become mesmerized by a family of friends when they show up to youth group. Somehow it takes away the sting of a broken family life at home. Over the years, I have gauged the crowd in our youth ministries. I cannot ever remember a time when more than half of the students came from a traditional classic home with both biological parents. I'm not saying blended homes are always a negative. That is far from the case. But the youth ministry can be a great example of a healthy family.

One more thing I want to address in this family approach to youth ministry is the growing demonic issue of *human trafficking*. The lure of sex traffickers plays right into this acceptance and relationship vacuum in a teenager's life by appealing to them at their surface level first ("You are so beautiful," or "You must be eighteen or nineteen" to a younger target) and then at the felt-need level ("We have a great big family," "We are all so close," or "You could make a lot of money").

> *A young teenager who is struggling at home or not fitting in with the right crowd can be easily wooed by the traffickers' pitch to join their awesome group or family that will take care of them. That is why it is so important to build healthy conversations and relationships with teens and to love them with an unconditional extravagant love in the youth ministry. I never want our students to look elsewhere for the brotherly love and acceptance they need.*

No doubt human trafficking is one of the more tragic outcomes of our dysfunctional family life, church, society, and sexuality.

7. AN INTEGRATION MINDSET

There is a tension between the church and the unchurched or unsaved person. It's a tension that's much easier to address than we have made it.

We need to *celebrate* people before they are *civilized*; we must allow people to *belong* before they *behave*.

In this statement, notice the emphasis on the person and not on any issue, struggle, or sin condition they might have. Here is an easy way to illustrate this: I have watched pious and self-righteous Christians who point their fingers at certain people yet throw their hands in the air and jump up and down to celebrate their favorite athlete when they score a touchdown. Even though that athlete may not be a believer. I have watched sanctimonious Christians who will cuddle up to wealthy people...yet have no time for the poor.

It is important that we *celebrate* people before they are *civilized*. That we allow people to *belong* before they *behave*. Great. But what does that mean exactly?

This means allowing *uncivilized* (whatever that means) people to be involved in the church. It means allowing *misbehaved* (whatever that means) people to be included in the church. For example, we allow many people who are not living a lifestyle that is pleasing to God to be involved and included in the church. Because they have a *lesser sin* than those who are not *civilized* or *behaving*, they are given a pass to be part of the church and its ministry. That is partiality, as we said earlier. And partiality is a sin.

Let me explain more directly.

I understand the difference between *leading programs* and *leading people*.

> *For instance, there must be a standard of conduct and maturity for people to be in a position of authority over others. However, I am much less concerned about the conduct and maturity of those who are simply involved in programs.*

Specifically, we should allow for *involvement* and *inclusion* of the *uncivilized* and *misbehaving*—by our standards, not theirs—in matters where they are not *leading* people in worship from the platform, in small group instruction, or preaching. I believe if we are going to practice as Christ did, we must allow the *uncivilized* and *misbehaved* to greet in the parking lot or at the door, usher or host in our services, work in tech ministry, and an array of other *program*-oriented avenues of *involvement* and *inclusion*. There is a higher responsibility in the church for who we allow to lead *people* versus who we allow to be involved in *programs*.

This is not perfect inclusion but it is a huge step in the right direction.

8. A COMPASSIONATE MINDSET

In the past year, *Teen Vogue*, *TIME*, *Rolling Stone*, *Sports Illustrated*, and *National Geographic* have all covered their magazines and websites with reports on the sexual revolution. The following statistics have been taken from these sources. The details of this generation are astounding actually—for the good and the bad. This is the world teenagers are growing up in. Feast and famine! Looking at the world of teenagers today is like seeing through a prism or a kaleidoscope. It is beautifully and spectacularly messy and hard to figure out or comprehend.

The findings are remarkable:

- 76 percent of Christian teens believe gender is your birth sex
- 48 percent of all Gen Z believe gender is your birth sex
- 77 percent of students experience physical, mental, or verbal abuse in high school
- One in three girls is abused by a boyfriend
- Seven out of ten high school seniors have had oral sex

And yet:

- 96 percent of evangelical teens do not believe it is okay for teens to have sex
- 50 percent fewer teenagers have driven while intoxicated than ten years ago
- 50 percent fewer teenagers are smoking than ten years ago
- Fewer teens are sexually active now than twenty years ago
- Teen pregnancy is at an all-time low
- The high school dropout rate is at an all-time low

Why all of this? What does this prove? It proves that cultural morality hasn't worked. Cultural progressive, personal, humanistic ideology produces changing morality and spiraling statistics. It never will be able to replace the absolutes of Scripture. But rising above these stats, it also proves there is a glimmer of hope for the church. That in the midst of the darkness, there is a desire for something more deep down in the heart of this generation.

> *This is an important time in history. The church's response to an unbelieving world is critical to the world's response to the faith in the church.*

When is the last time you cried for a teenager? When is the last time you listened without speaking, judging, or trying to fix someone? What is our compassion level for people? Are we surprised or shocked or cynical or isolating toward people who think differently than we do? Or are we unflinching, understanding, and empathetic when hearing about a lifestyle or point of view from someone who does not think as we do?

We do not have to shed our truth at the door of relationship. Love values relationship without throwing out the regulations. Love values people without throwing out the principles. Love values friendships without having to win arguments. Compassion has a unique way of treating people with both truth and love at the same time.

Remember, this generation does not go to church. They have not clearly heard the gospel of Jesus Christ. If asked their faith perspective, they have none. We do not need to *reintroduce* Jesus to teenagers. We need to *introduce* Jesus to them—because they do not know who He is. This is the world we live in. Yet if teenagers are *asked* to go to church, they will.

Do our students see us crying over their friends? Do our students see us praying for their friends? Have our students heard us speak compassionately about their friends? Our students are learning how to treat their friends by our response as leaders to their friends. *And that turns them into kings and queens!*

9. A PRACTICAL MINDSET

I remember when I first started youth ministry, my late wife told me I was too deep. She once remarked, "I'm so glad you love the kids because you cannot preach." She told me my preaching was too deep and the only reason the students were coming was because they loved me. Yep.

In our approach to youth ministry, we can spend a lot of time on *theory* and information while spending little time on *practices* and application. However, there must be a balance between the *theoretical* and the *practical* so our students can learn to apply what they've been taught. It is not enough to tell them what's right and what's wrong, what they should or should not do. We need to help our students *make the faith their own*.

I want to give you a short list of the scriptural framework we have used in this book to help your students build a Christian worldview and deal with the sexual revolution. Make sure you review the next chapter on *tough questions*, which offers more practical help on how to deal with sexuality.

Scriptural Framework

- Genesis 1–3: a theology of firsts and the creation design of male and female and family

- Deuteronomy 23:17–18: the prohibition of sexual sin

- Proverbs 5–10: Solomon details the wisdom of fleeing the dangers of sexual temptation

- Matthew 15:19–20: Jesus on sins such as adultery and sexual immorality

- Matthew 19: Jesus's support of the Mosaic law and intent for marriage

- Romans 1: the process of deception and a clear definition of illicit sexual behavior

- 1 Corinthians 6:9–11: unnatural sexual behavior and the possibility of transformation

- Galatians 5:19–26: the *lusts* of the flesh and the *lists* of the Spirit

- 1 Thessalonians 4:4: how to possess your vessel in purity

- 1 Timothy 1:9–11: the lawless acts of sexual behaviors

- Hebrews 13:4: the purpose of singularity and purity in marriage

- Jude 4–7: Jude's review of the Genesis 19 story of Sodom and Gomorrah

- Revelation 22:15: a list of transgressors kept outside of the gates of heaven

If our students can understand what the Scriptures say about sexuality, they will have a stronger ability to defend and define their faith to their peers.

We can remove the fear or the question of where Christians stand on the issues from the minds of our students if we provide basic biblical instruction. We must develop our scriptural framework of the issues in the youth service, in small groups, in our mentoring, in the way we model family, and even through guest speakers. These settings are a critical place to raise students with good spiritual formation and biblical standards. Scripture is our source and our relevance to this generation in addressing the sexual revolution in America.

The *principles* of one generation become the *practices* of the next.

10. THE LOVE MINDSET

The preface to this book opened with the concept of *God is Love*. In the second chapter, we saw that the devil stole sex when he stole love. In the chapter on theology, we defined love as the theological center for sexuality. In the chapter on social sexuality, we explored how love is missing in our culture. In the family chapter, we stressed the importance of the family placing a guard of love around their children. And in this chapter on youth leadership, we've examined how the unconditional power of the youth ministry can appeal to our teenagers and guard them from a conditional world.

> *I hope you have seen the love revolution throughout this book. The love revolution could be the answer to this tsunami called the sexual revolution in America. I have no doubt that a massive love revolution could wash away the debris that was dumped on our shores by this last sexual revolution.*

The love approach provides an easy *agree-to-disagree* mindset.

One of the most mature responses we can have to a person we disagree with is to *agree to disagree*. Especially as it relates to morality issues. Truth and love are important partners in our relationship with people. If you cannot love, then stay away from issues that divide until you can agree to disagree. We do not have to shed our truth at the door of relationship.

I believe when you love, you can hold tightly to truth and grace at the same time.

The MTV Video Music Awards

Something happened a few years ago while I was watching the Video Music Awards (VMA) show. These awards are the barometer of our teen culture and the producers of teen life in America. You may not like it, but it's true. For its biggest show of the year, which takes place at the end of the summer, MTV parades its pop stars and messages to millions of teens as a forerunner to the beginning of the school year and the social conversations that will spread the media giant's message through the teen world overnight.

Listen, I love a good party. The VMA show's energy was like many great church services I have been in. Did you catch that? The creativity was at its height. Is there a better set design on TV? For the most part, the costumes—because we all *know* they don't wear that stuff offstage—were fun to see. And there was actually *some* talent. Seriously, the secular artists today have *nothing* on the talent in the church.

But taking a step back from the initial anger and shock, what was actually being promoted? Sex and rebellion against authority.

What I found interesting was a very graphic moment in the middle of the evening and the Will Smith family's response to it. As one of the performing artists became quite sexually graphic and obscene, the camera panned to Will Smith and his family, sitting in the front row. The entire family looked at each other in shock. I wish MTV had shown more responses throughout the crowd. Because I really believe that deep down inside, our society knows when we have crossed the line.

What I saw in the response of the Will Smith family was a willingness to stand against what was being done, while keeping a relationship with the people around them at the same time. Over the years, I have watched other examples of this, but that night was particularly encouraging to me. Since then, I have thought many times about my response as a youth pastor to the sexual revolution in America today. I have wondered, *What do my students who are watching me see in my life in the face of the sexual revolution?* I hope they see my embarrassment as well as my compassion.

FINALLY

If a guy is a good worshipper, that's what I'm attracted to!
—Desiree, age 15

Kings and queens are not born. *Princes and princesses are born; kings and queens are made.* Our love for God and our love for man is attractive to this world. The youth ministry that does both of these well will explode with growth. When we disciple students and create a setting for teenagers to worship God with their whole heart and love their neighbor as they do themselves, the atmosphere will be charged with appeal. People talk about attractional ministry all the time. I can't think of anything much more attractive than young people in love with God and each other!

> *Given the conditional acceptance that exists in this world, a youth ministry that loves unconditionally will have no lack of growth. In too many homes, schools, social groups, work, sports teams, and other settings, the world loves conditionally. The conditional motto is: if you...then I will. Teenagers are tired of conditional love and acceptance. When the youth ministry loves unconditionally, look out. Both the churched and the unchurched will be there.*

As youth leaders, we have a great responsibility to prepare the next generation theologically and not just culturally. This is how we should be evaluating our ministry. I measure my work by the theological preparedness of teenagers. It may be easy to assess your work by looking at *attendance, energy, social media interaction, hype levels, events, merchandise,* and *feedback.* But we cannot lose the importance of preparing the next generation theologically. This is our critical function.

A truism often misattributed to Edmund Burke goes like this: *"The only thing necessary for the triumph of evil is for good men to do nothing."*

We are modeling to our students how they should respond to their world. God has not called us to hide behind our message and point fingers at people who may be different from us. Please don't judge the person who may have different views than you. Respect them. And correct them when you can. Because if someone does not correct the excesses of one generation, the next generation will take it to another level.

We are the good men and women who have something to say about the sexual revolution. Are we sending our students into the wild with truth and grace? Do our students have everything they need to speak into the sexual revolution happening right before their eyes? This is our role as youth leaders. Do not get sidetracked with lesser things. Theology is the disciple-making process of Christianity that will help our students handle any topic in their life and their world.

In too many cases, if sexuality is even discussed in the youth setting, it is done with a pick-and-choose *meology* or a cultural approach. With thoughts, ideas, and opinions from a youth leader who feels somewhat incapable of parsing the theological application to the topic or issue. But what is needed most in youth leadership is a *theology* approach. Where youth leaders with a base of biblical knowledge and understanding are able to communicate so that students are interested in the Scriptures.

There must be a renewed theological sexuality education in youth ministry.

> *The reform we need in America will not come from the changing legislation in government, the lack of censorship in the media, the progressive sex education in our schools, or the redefinition of family. It will come from youth leaders who are shaping the next generation in America with another sexual revolution of biblical proportions.* **A biblical sexual revolution**.

Like the proverbial *ant in front of the train*, we will not be able to stand against the sexual revolution and its tsunami of influence and change washing over our society unless we respond with both truth and grace. The sexual revolution isn't going away any time soon. But even though one generation has brought a tsunami of unrighteousness crashing over our culture, I believe another generation can start an equally powerful *tsunami of righteousness*. With the same kind of influence and overwhelming change.

As youth leaders, our approach to sexuality in this generation is critical. Our clarity of theology and willingness to stand against culture is critical. With the ever-changing sexual revolution in our world comes a chasm of distance between the church and culture. This separation can be avoided. And it *must* be avoided. Especially by youth leaders who are shaping the sexuality ethic of the next generations who will be leading the church into its greatest days ahead of us.

We can counter *the sexual revolution* crashing over our society, but it will take a tsunami of consistently modeled biblical truth and love. *The love revolution* that our students can bring to this world if we prepare them.

Your relationships are drawing a picture each day for nonbelievers around you of who God really is. Which kind of picture are you drawing?
—Jeanne Mayo, veteran youth pastor

The depravity of man is at once the most empirically verifiable reality, but at the same time, the most intellectually resisted fact.   —Malcolm Muggeridge

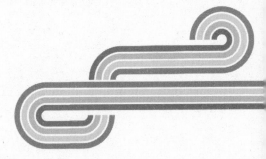

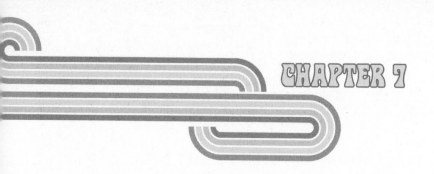

WINNING ARGUMENTS AND LOSING FRIENDSHIPS
Answering Tough Questions

I don't want the answers to questions nobody is asking. But answering these tough questions brings a lot of division. Mostly because we cannot decide upon an absolute moral base of what is right and wrong.

Muggeridge nailed it, didn't he? What a thought with which to start this last chapter. The fact that our own depravity, and the depravity of humankind, is undeniable. Except in our own minds.

It is easy for us to admit the existence of sin in someone else's life. But an entirely different reality when it comes to ourselves. Why? Because over the course of our lifetime, we place others on trial and play the prosecutor, while at the same time, we defend ourselves.

It will be difficult for this chapter to be successful unless we have a clear definition of sin. That's right, there *is* such a thing as sin. It's almost as if we need a new introduction of the definition of sin into our culture because we simply do not understand, or agree on, what sin actually is. Although it is not popular in our society to label a certain behavior as sin, or to call someone a sinner, there is the reality of sin as defined in the Bible.

MISSING THE MARK

In the twenty-first century, we have come up with comfortable names for our sin.

We don't even *think* of it as sin. Instead, we call it a *weakness*, or my *struggle*, or our *issue*. It has become popular to call sin by more palatable names such as *addictions*, or *habits*, or even *dispositions*. All of us have certain inclinations to think, do, or say things we shouldn't. All of us were born in sin. But being born in sin is simply the truest argument for the need to be born again.

If I hear one more person say, "*That's just the way I am,*" or "*I was born that way,*" as an excuse for their behavior, I'm gonna lose my mind. At some point, we must face our disobedient actions and thoughts and call them what they are—sin.

Or *missing the mark.*

That's the actual definition of sin. The Greek word is *hamartia*, which means to *miss the mark*, or *to be guilty* or *at fault for not hitting the target*, according to *Strong's Concordance*. It can be interpreted as self-originated deeds. In an ethical sense, it means failure, a sinful deed. Whoever has sinned is guilty. Just reading that definition is difficult to hear, isn't it? But it is very clear.

> *It is also clear in the Bible that forgiveness or atonement for sin means to repent of our sin and* **stop** *the pattern, or the disposition, or the weakness, or the habit, or the addiction, or the deed, or the behavior.* **To actually stop our sinning in a certain area.**

It's hard to completely understand why people have such a difficult time with the word *sin*. As sinners, when I look at the relationship of God our Creator and we His children, it is remarkable. He sees us graciously through the eyes of Christ, even though, in fact, we are still sinners. But then I look at the relationship between the church and humanity and I understand a little better why the world has a hard time with this concept of sin. I believe it is because the church sees the world as sinners rather than seeing humanity through the eyes of Christ. Maybe this is why people have such a difficult time with the word *sin*—because the church does not see them graciously through the eyes of Christ.

THE ROMANS ROAD AND FAITH WORKS

Let's look quickly at two concepts to consider in this chapter: *the Romans Road* and *Faith Works*.

THE ROMANS ROAD

The Romans Road is often called *the Sinner's Prayer* for the use of leading someone to faith in Christ. It has been used for many years to explain the simple ABCs of salvation: *admit*, *believe*, and *confess*.

Admit

Everyone has sinned and is far away from God's saving presence.
(Romans 3:23 GNT)

This means everyone has sinned against God's standard, or target, or mark, or His commands. No one is exempt.

Believe

For sin pays its wage—death; but God's free gift is eternal life in union with Christ Jesus our Lord.   (Romans 6:23 GNT)

This means when we miss the mark, there are consequences—spiritual and ultimately eternal death if we do not receive God's forgiveness or atonement for our sin.

And finally:

Confess

> *If you confess that Jesus is Lord and believe that God raised him from death, you will be saved.* **For it is by our faith that we are put right with God; it is by our confession that we are saved.** (Romans 10:9–10 GNT)

This last verse is powerful because it involves the entire ABCs of salvation in one sentence. It is up to us to *admit* our sin, *believe* in our hearts that Christ can forgive us from that sin, and *confess* with our mouth that Jesus is Lord moving forward over that area.

FAITH WORKS

James was a kinsman of Jesus—brother or cousin or some other close relative. Can you imagine that? That would be some kind of pressure, being related to the perfect Son of God! In his letter to the twelve tribes, James talks about salvation. The *Faith Works* passages create a balance between our faith and our works or actions. We cannot simply believe; we must also behave. A true born again experience will result in a changed life. That is what repentance is, a 180-degree change. In other words, we do not only *ask* for change, but we *act* like we are changed.

James asks two important questions:

> *Dear friends, do you think you'll get anywhere in this if you learn all the right words but never do anything?* (James 2:14)

Isn't it obvious that God-talk without God-acts is outrageous non-sense?   (James 2:17)

James gives us the examples of how faith and works go together. And in verse 24, he makes his point of salvation a balance when he says, *"Is it not evident that a person is made right with God not by a barren faith but by faith fruitful in works?"*

Let's look at the forgiveness of sin and being born again one more way.

I think we would all agree that when we break a civil or moral law, we are guilty or have *missed the mark*. In other words, we have sinned against the government (in the civil sense) or God (in the moral sense). We may not like or agree with the law, but we have broken it anyway. In the civil sense, when this happens, the consequences of breaking the law are paying a fine for what we have done or going to jail.

> *In the spiritual sense, when we break the law, miss the mark, or fall short of the target, the fine has already been paid! We simply need to ask God to apply the paid fee of Christ on the cross to our sins by asking for forgiveness, believing in our hearts that it's been given, and stop doing the deed!*

I think most of us would agree the Ten Commandments must not be broken because they are universally accepted as God's standard. But even the Ten Commandments have some detractors. Of course, there are a few commandments that no one would argue with; murder, being unfaithful to your spouse, stealing, and lying are all considered unacceptable behavior. But not everyone in America today would agree that idolatry, breaking the Sabbath rest, or coveting are wrong.

This is where it becomes complicated, when we disagree on what it means to sin or *miss the mark*.

As a Christian, my framework for right and wrong, or my worldview and box, is formed from the Scriptures—*an unchanging absolute over time*. A non-Christian will build their box or framework for right or wrong and their worldview from, among other things, a culture that's *changing relative with the times*. Now, I realize even Christians will disagree on my interpretation of the Scriptures, but I will attempt to be as true in my exegesis as I can to answer these questions from a clearly biblical perspective and not only my personal perspective.

With that said, I like tension. Tension is undervalued.

> *The following questions and answers in this chapter will evoke agreement and disagreement from my readers. For a variety of reasons. Maybe someone does not hold to my interpretation of the Scriptures on a certain topic, or maybe someone does not **want** to accept that interpretation. I'm sure others will not even care about the Scriptures as a basis for answering these questions.*

Since we have already had commentary on several key passages in the theology section relating to these questions—Genesis 1–3; Proverbs; the messianic narrative in Matthew 5, 15, and 19; Paul's narrative in Romans 1 and 1 Corinthians 6–7; the words of Peter in 2 Peter 2; and Jude chapter 1—we'll stick with common-sense application of the Scriptures here to respond briefly to each of these questions. I will also do a little commentary from a few other passages that relate to each question.

As we look at these questions and responses, remember what Malcolm Muggeridge, the English journalist, theologian, and spy, said at the beginning of this chapter: "The depravity of man is at once the most empirically verifiable reality, but at the same time, the most intellectually resisted fact."

May we try not to prosecute others and defend ourselves, but may we allow God that duty.

> True freedom isn't the right to do what you want.
> Instead it's the power to do what you should.
> —Jeanne Mayo, veteran youth pastor

QUESTION #1

CAN A PERSON WHO PRACTICES (PATTERNS) SIN IN THEIR LIFE BE A BORN-AGAIN CHRISTIAN?

No. For several reasons. Paul said in Romans 6, Galatians 5, and 1 Corinthians that if we practice sin, we cannot inherit the kingdom of God. Foremost, however, *calling* yourself a Christian does not *make* you a Christian. As we have seen, you must believe and turn from your sin to be born again. It requires faith *and* works. At the point when you are willingly practicing a known sin, you have missed the mark. Confession is only part of salvation. It is Dietrich Bonhoeffer's description of cheap and costly grace. Cheap grace is repentance without obedience to Christ. Costly grace is repentance and obedience to Christ.

This may be one of the most difficult questions to answer. This has become the moment of contention between the church and the unchurched on all matters of life. And yet there are several very clear Scriptures that seem to answer this question quite easily. Let's look at this as simply as we can. Here is an important concept if we are going to answer this question:

You do not have to behave to belong.

Maybe you've heard this popular statement in the argument between the church and culture. I've used it. Especially when it comes to my relationship with lost people. Far too many people have laid out a list of behaviors people must keep before they're allowed to belong. But I do not want people to think they have to get cleaned up in order to come to Christ or seek Him in the church. For someone to belong in a relationship with me or the church is quite loose for me. It's called mercy and grace.

But belonging to the kingdom and to Christ is another step. That requires both belief and behavior. And it requires us to get cleaned up.

Remember the thief on the cross who asked Jesus to remember him when He entered His kingdom? (See Luke 23:40–43.) He had lived a criminal's life, but in one moment, he was escorted into heaven by Jesus and His grace. He didn't have a lot of time to get cleaned up and act a certain way. But what we do know is that whatever patterns he was committing at the time, even just for a moment, he repented of those. So there's hope for all of us!

I love what Paul told the Galatians:

> *You foolish Galatians! Who put a spell on you? Before your very eyes you had a clear description of the death of Jesus Christ on the cross!...You began by God's Spirit; do you now want to finish by your own power?*   (Galatians 3:1, 3 GNT)

This is a great challenge for each of us to remember that Christianity is costly grace and not cheap grace. It requires God's grace and our obedience.

The Author of Lists

In Romans 6:16–23, Galatians 5:16–21, and 1 Corinthians 6:9–12, Paul describes the uncontrollable lust of the flesh with a list of sins and their consequences. Now Paul was an author of lists. There was no confusion in Paul's writings on any topic because he would write very clearly, using many examples or lists to make a point. Look at the many lists Paul shared in his writings in the New Testament:

- The qualities of love in 1 Corinthians 13

- His hardships and sufferings in 2 Corinthians 11

- Fruit of the flesh in Galatians 5 and 1 Corinthians 6

- Fruit of the Spirit in Galatians 5

- Paul lists about twenty-one gifts of the Spirit throughout the New Testament in Romans, Corinthians, and (perhaps) Hebrews

So to be clear, when Paul is writing, he is conscious of including examples for us with whatever topic he is addressing. I believe Paul does this for clarity.

These texts in Romans 6, Galatians 5, and 1 Corinthians 6 have some very real language that must be dealt with when it comes to answering this question—can a person who practices sin be a born-again Christian?—about all kinds of unbiblical behavior. Understand here, Paul is not just dealing with sexual sins in these passages. In all, Paul lists about twenty-three different prohibitions and adds the words *"things like these"* (Galatians 5:21 GNT). That is inclusive. He is comprehensively speaking of uncontrollable sins and enumerating several sins ranging from adultery and fornication to dissension, heresy, idolatry, hatred, and murder.

The Author of Clarity

Now, if our motto for life is *anything goes*, then these passages sound legalistic and unfair. What a killjoy God must be. That is how some view Christianity. But let's look at it another way. Instead of seeing Christianity as a killjoy with do's and don'ts, why not look at it as safety and clarity and a box?

> *Consider seeing Christianity as you would civil law. I think we can all agree that traffic laws, for example, are necessary and save lives. Without speed limits, traffic signals, or signs, there would be chaos on our roads and highways. We would be risking our lives every time we ventured out.*

In the same manner, how would you feel about living in a world where there were *no* rules?

Let's say that for one week, civil law was suspended in America. What if it wasn't illegal for people to break in and enter your home? Or for shoppers to take whatever food they want at the grocery store for free? Or for media outlets to publish slander and untruths about you and not be held accountable? These kinds of universal codes or laws bring order to a society. Can you imagine living in a free world without a set of universal standards and civil ordinances to guide our actions and behaviors?

> *This is what God set up for humanity in the Scriptures: a universal framework for behavior and deciding what is right and wrong.*

God is not a killjoy; in the Bible, He has simply given us a framework with which to guide our lives. Sure, there are civil and ceremonial laws and analogies that people point to in the Bible and label as unrealistic or absurd. But those instances must be read within the context they were written and for the moment they were intended. You may not agree with biblical laws—the same way you may not agree with civil laws—but the Scriptures give us a set of standards to guide our actions and behaviors. And if we do not submit to these biblical codes or laws, there are consequences, just as there are consequences when we disobey civil codes or laws.

Unknown Practices

Reading my Bible changes my thinking.
—Allie, age 19

The difficulty with this question is when we get into unknown or unrevealed sin. Deception.

There is another important lesson in these passages. By using a comprehensive list of prohibitions, Paul is making it clear that no one should rush to judgment of another person who has committed a certain prohibition different from their own sin. Because of the comprehensive list, there is no room for focusing upon one sin more often than another.

> It can be easy to look critically at the certain culturally popular sexual sins, such as adultery, fornication, and sexual immorality, and place greater emphasis and judgment upon these prohibitions. At the same time, we miss the other sins that are more prevalent in our society, such as stealing, drunkenness, hatred, gossip, and jealousy—especially when these exist in our own life.

Deception or unknown sin is certainly a part to play thanks to our sinful nature. Romans 1 and 6, as well as Psalm 51, deal with our lean toward sin. Maybe you've heard someone say, "I am just biologically conditioned naturally to same-sex attraction (or alcoholism or anger). God must have made me this way. I have asked Him to take it away but He hasn't."

There are two responses that I have to this argument or excuse.

First, if you are going to use your *nature* as an excuse for the argument, then allow *God's nature* to be used against your argument, too. That is, male and female were designed by God *naturally* as binary gender and complementary to each other's bodies for sex within marriage.

Second, some people use the argument that they have asked God to take their sin away, but after praying, they still have the desires. So, they reason, "God must not care about my condition." Well, there are two ways for God to answer that kind of prayer:

1. He can **deliver** you instantly by His power and set you free from whatever you are asking freedom from.

2. Or, you can **discipline** yourself from whatever you are asking freedom from through reading the Word, worshipping, praying, fasting, discipleship, and accountability.

Many of us would prefer God to *deliver* us from temptation rather than for us to *discipline* ourselves from temptation. David said all of us were born into sin (see Psalm 51) and Paul said that we must die to our sinful nature and be *born again* unto life (see Romans 8). This is the idea of celibate gay Christians who struggle with the desire for a same-sex relationship but recognize it to be unnatural and a sin against God's natural order. And while they wait for the freedom from their flesh, they deliver themselves in their spirit through discipline!

One more thing about desires. Remember, in Genesis 2–3, desire was an evil thing when it was not for the right thing. Desire can become deadly unless we can control it. A proper theology of God does not allow us to fit Scripture into our behaviors or desires; it requires us to fit our behavior or desires into the principles of the Scriptures. We must understand their authority.

The Bible does not categorize our humanity by our sexual desires—or any other desire.
—Christopher Yuan, Bible professor and author

The Author of Consequence

To be specific in answering the question of whether someone can continue in sin and still be born again, after listing prohibitions or sins, Paul uses final consequential phrases to encourage us to avoid them:

> *Work hard for sin your whole life and your pension is death.*
> (Romans 6:23)

> *If you use your freedom this way, you will not inherit God's king-dom.*   (Galatians 5:21)

> *If I went around doing whatever I thought I could get by with, I'd be a slave to my whims.*   (1 Corinthians 6:12)

Aside from the thorough description of this unnatural behavior, there is the warning of the consequences for breaking these codes or laws and *missing the mark*.

To be *born again* is to be dead to the old works and alive to the new works. When we give our life to Christ, salvation is immediate (justification). But it doesn't stop there. Discipleship is the process whereby we go through a transformation, resulting in holiness and maturity (sanctification). I do not believe we can practice or pattern known sin and be born again. The point at which someone knowingly is disobedient to Scripture is a point of sin and must be repented of immediately.

QUESTION #2

IS HAVING SEX BEFORE MARRIAGE A SIN?

Yes. But not only that, by all accounts and research, it really isn't smart.

My parents taught me that Christmas morning was so much better when everything was a surprise. So, I want my honeymoon to be a surprise!

—Juan, age 16

There are many verses that define the prohibition against sex before marriage throughout the Old and New Testaments. As we have said in the chapter on theology, Genesis 1–3 defines the design and parameters of God for sexuality, and Proverbs 5–10 is filled with warnings about sex outside of marriage. We can also look to Jesus in Matthew 5, 15, and 19; Paul in 1 Corinthians 6–7, Romans 1, and 1 Thessalonians 4; Peter in 2 Peter; Jude and the accusations against Sodom and Gomorrah; and John in Revelation 2, 18, 19, and 22. There are other Scriptures on the dangers of sexual sin, but these will suffice.

Throughout these texts, this topic is tied to our sanctification and maturity; it is tied to adultery, idolatry, prostitution or whoredom, and lust, and it is tied to the kind of uncleanness and revelry leading up to promiscuous sex. To answer this specific question, we will use our texts from Paul from the first question (Galatians 5 and 1 Corinthians 6–7) because we have an understanding already of what the Scriptures are saying.

> It's clear that sex outside of marriage between a man and woman is prohibited by Scripture. Hebrews 13:4 stresses, "Honor marriage, and guard the sacredness of sexual intimacy between wife and husband. God draws a firm line against casual and illicit sex." Looking at the whole of Scripture, there simply is no theological or common-sense argument around this.

This question and topic is covered quite clearly in Galatians 5 and 1 Corinthians 6–7. One of the words that is used for sex outside of marriage here, and in most of these other texts, is the word *porneia*, or fornication. As we mentioned in the theology chapter, the word literally means sexual uncleanness such as unchastity, sexual immorality, illicit sexual intercourse or impurity, and willingly selling off or surrendering virginity. Fornication is also used in the plural sense as the collection of multiple sexual sins.

The boundaries of Scripture are clear. God is love and God is holy. The great part about this is the forgiveness of our sins if we break His words and miss the mark. There are always consequences for our behavior outside of biblical standards, but there is always a remission of our sins when we are repentant. And that gives us a new start and a second chance.

> I didn't wait. But I'm so glad I get another chance to wait. The way I see it, I can't rewrite my past, but I can write my future.
> —Hope, age 18

In answering this question, it is clear many authors in the Bible used or referenced the word *porneia* as a broad and inclusive word for many actions. Jesus and Paul were two who used this word most often in the New Testament. It included illicit, unnatural sexual immoralities, thoughts, and behaviors that are contrary to God's physical and spiritual design for human sexuality.

QUESTION #3

IS HOMOSEXUALITY A SIN?

No. Having homosexual feelings and attractions is not a sin.

Yes. The act of homosexuality is a sin.

Please understand, same-sex *attraction* is not sin. Same-sex *action* is sin.

The disposition or feeling of homosexual attraction is not a sin on its own. It is when the person acts upon it, when that feeling becomes action, that homosexuality is a sin. Being tempted is not a sin. It is when we act upon the temptation that we have missed the mark.

> *There are believing celibate gay Christians who understand their inclination toward homosexual acts is sin. Out of commitment to Christ, they have chosen not to engage in sex outside of marriage or same-sex relations. I know many of them are waiting for the church to embrace them and allow them to not just attend church, but also be involved and share in ministry.*

Let's put it another way: suppose you need a new phone charger. You see one in a store and no one else is around. *You get the feeling that you could just take the charger* and walk out without paying for it. If you deny the disposition or the feeling, you have not stolen. But if you don't buy the charger and just take it, then you are stealing.

To use another example, if you are eating lunch with friends, you may *have the disposition or get the feeling to gossip, exaggerate, or lie about another person.* If you deny that disposition or feeling and do not spread the rumor about that person, you are not sinning in that way.

The answers to the first two questions provide a lot of theological work and clarity that could also be used here. But let's use a couple of other principles in relation to this question now.

Since we have already reviewed commentary on several key passages in the theology section on this question—Genesis 1–3; the messianic narrative in Matthew 15 and 19; Paul's narrative in Romans 1; the words of Peter in 2 Peter 2; and the letter of Jude— let me stay with arguments of common sense here to respond briefly to this question.

Moses's Creation Narrative

There is no confusion about God's design and intent of male or female gender, His design for marriage, or His design of sexual relations in Scripture. There is no allowance in the Scriptures for nonbinary categories, a *third way*, *transition*, or *neutral* gender. No marriage consent outside of a husband and wife. And there is no unbounded free sexual behavior between men and women or same-sex relations. In biblical cases of transgender or nonbinary language, where marriage was not honored between a man and a woman, and free sexual behavior was practiced, the Bible is clearly not condoning these things, but merely speaking of their existence. Whether that included eunuchs, kings taking multiple wives, temple prostitutes, or idolatrous sexual relations, this foundational sexuality intent of Genesis is very clear:

There are to be no sexual relations outside of marriage or with the same gender.

Jesus's Narrative in Matthew 5, 15, and 19

Furthermore, look at Jesus's words again. The problem of homosexuality was far out of the mainstream for the Jews. It just wasn't a question of conduct for them. That is why the references to same-sex relations are mentioned clearly but sparingly in the Bible. The practice was seen by all to be outside of human sexual design. Homosexual acts were rare in Jewish society and ultimately their writing reflects this.

> *And yet some will attempt critical thinking around the idea that Jesus didn't spend a lot of time addressing homosexuality—or any other sexual issue, for that matter—by specific terminology or name, so He must not be against it. Using this same line of thinking, bestiality was never specifically mentioned in the New Testament either, but I'm sure you are not thinking that it must be okay. Just*

> *because the mythological gods displayed such behavior*
> *doesn't make it right for us.*

This idea of the prevalence or frequency of an issue determining its stated importance doesn't make sense to me. Are we going to create our theology of anything on how often the issue is dealt with? Jesus spoke of adultery, sexual immorality, and fornication about sixteen times. Is that not enough? Maybe we too, like the Jews, should have a minimalist view on this and other issues because a proper common sense expression of sexuality is understood without trying to make a case for it.

> *Jesus clearly assumed in His language and treatment of*
> *homosexuality and other sexual sins that these were not in*
> *line with the design of human sexuality. Especially if you*
> *interpret the words He used for sexual relations outside of*
> *marriage between a man and a woman as a prohibition.*

Let me say it this way:

- Jesus talked more about hell than love. Does that mean love isn't important?

- Jesus talked more about the Holy Spirit than money. Does that mean money isn't important?

- Jesus talked more about judging people than murder. Does that mean murder isn't important?

- Jesus talked more about the devil than the disciples. Does that mean the disciples aren't important?

The most important thing to remember about Jesus's words was His clarity.

Paul's Narrative in the Epistles

One thing that cannot be argued about Paul was his deep conviction about adherence to the Scriptures and our personal holiness. But with this comes much cultural judgment upon the church for crimes of association.

Let me explain. Many have argued that the church claims to believe in a Bible that is inerrant and infallible, and yet it contains many outdated and radical thoughts. I understand this and have also read these kinds of dark and tragic stories in Scripture. Yet if we take the Scriptures in their context and meaning, within their intended purposes, then all of the issues about inerrancy and infallibility can be answered. There are some things in Scripture that are simply civil law, cultural codes, war and military agreements, or analogies. Some of these kinds of narratives in Scripture have nothing to do with our society today. They were simply part of the history the Bible details but does not condone. And they are not meant to become practice today.

We must take the emotion out of the question and deal with the facts.

Because we have commented on the theology of the Greek word *arsenokoitai* already, let's do a simple review of 1 Corinthians 6:9 here.

It is important to look at the words that Paul uses in his text. The word Paul chooses is not steeped in tradition or common use. For that reason, it means so much more. Outside of the Bible's natural and creative definition of sexuality, *arsenokoitai* may be the most important word to use IN our discussion.

As a compound word, *arsenokoitai* is broken into the following: *arseno* is the word for "a male," and *koitai* is the word for "mat" or "bed." Put the two halves together, and the word means *a male bed*—that is, a person who makes use of *a male-only bed* or *a bed for males*. And, truthfully, that's all the information we need to understand the intent of Paul's choice of this word.

The Greek word *koitai* meaning "bed" carries a sexual connotation in this context. This word is the source of our English word *coitus* ("sexual intercourse"). The conclusion is that Paul's use of the word *arsenokoitai* is referring to homosexuals—men who are in bed with other men, engaging in same-gender sexual activity.

Paul's use of terms is consistent throughout his writings as he uses synonyms for several of his words. As Robert Gagnon noted:

> The term "sexual uncleanness" (*akatharsia*) employed for same-sex intercourse appears later in [Romans] 6:19 as a synonym for the word "sin" (*hamartia*, 6:16–18, 20, 22–23). It usually occurs in conjunction with two other synonyms for sexual sins: *porneia* ("sexual immorality") and *aselgeia* ("licentiousness").[65]

Paul's use of words is very broad and conclusive.

> *Paul does not even hint at any notion that some homosexual relationships are acceptable. There is no emphasis on cultic sex practice, or whether love or committed same-sex relationships are exempt; there is no age allowance, no ownership/slavery stance, and no acceptance for sex outside of the marriage of a man and a woman. Paul's word was chosen as an overarching word for same-gender sex.*

Studying Paul's writings, here's what Church of England priest Peter Ould has to say about any confusion with this word:

> We can see that the argument that *arsenokoites* refers to a specific subset of homosexual activity (prostitution or cultic practices) cannot be supported by any of the post New Testament

---

65. Dr. Robert Gagnon, "The Apostle Paul on Sexuality: A Response," *LeadershipU Archives*, 2003, (www.leaderu.com/theology/paulandsexuality.html).

literature. We have established that *arsenokoites* first appears within the New Testament and therefore it is reasonable to assume that Paul either creates the word himself, or that it was created by the first Century Rabbinic community that Paul operated in (at least before his conversion). Given this, the most reasonable etymology is that the word is sourced from the [Greek Old Testament or *Septuagint*] LXX, where the verses that it comes from condemn all homosexual activity, or alternatively, a straight Greek translation of the Rabbinic *miskab zakur* [Hebrew for lying with a male]. This is supported by the clear first century Rabbinic teaching that condemned all homosexual activity regardless of context (and supporting teaching in the Babylonian Talmud and elsewhere).[66]

Let's move to another response to this question on homosexuality. There's much we have already said of the sins of Sodom and Gomorrah. You've heard my thoughts on this in the section on theology. Now, listen to Peter's and Jude's thoughts on Genesis 19 and Sodom and Gomorrah.

Peter's and Jude's Thoughts on Genesis 19

This text in Genesis 19 is so divisive, many people will not touch it. Let me take it from a different angle. Biblical hermeneutics, or proper interpretation of Scripture, requires sound textual criticism and sometimes includes external verification. So, let's see what two other writers bring to this controversial text on the question of homosexuality.

What is clear from Genesis 19:1–29 is that the sin of Sodom and Gomorrah was not singular.

---

66. Peter Ould, "Sexuality and Slavery – Part Three," July 12, 2009 (www.peter-ould. net/2009/07/12/sexuality-and-slavery-part-three).

I would agree with some of my friends who interpret this text to mean violence, rape, and not taking care of the poor and marginalized as among the reasons why God destroyed Sodom and Gomorrah. *But the uncleanness of homosexuality was clearly one of the reasons also.* Furthermore, even though some will use the Hebrew word *yada* in the text to mean these men simply wanted to talk and get to know the visitors, this word is also used for sexual relations. The broader context of the entire story is sexual dysfunction in Sodom and Gomorrah.

Peter references Genesis 19 quite clearly in his second epistle:

> *God decreed destruction for the cities of Sodom and Gomorrah. A mound of ashes was all that was left—grim warning to anyone bent on an ungodly life. But that good man Lot, driven nearly out of his mind by the sexual filth and perversity, was rescued. Surrounded by moral rot day after day after day, that righteous man was in constant torment. So God knows how to rescue the godly from evil trials. And he knows how to hold the feet of the wicked to the fire until Judgment Day. God is especially incensed against these "teachers" who live by lust, addicted to a filthy exis-tence.*   (2 Peter 2:6–10)

The context of these verses is almost exclusively about sexual sins. Peter was clearly saying the reason for the destruction of these two cities was not just homosexuality; it was many issues.

> *Of course, it was not simply for the sensual unrighteous acts of unprincipled men, but God was fed up with them for many things—incest, rape, violence, despising authority, and not taking care of the poor. And, as Peter says, homosexuality as well.*

Jude references Genesis 19 quite clearly also.

The angle of Peter and Jude from the New Testament is a clear view since they are familiar with the discussion and culture of Sodom and Gomorrah because the Roman Babylonian region was marked by sexual sins. When all the evidence from this story is considered, the traditional understanding is still the most consistent with the biblical criticism. It was common knowledge that Sodom, Gomorrah, and the surrounding areas gave themselves over to all sorts of sexual perversion (fornication), homosexual activity, and a desire for *strange flesh*.

Now, some have argued that phrase refers to the angels that were alluded to in the Genesis 19 story.

Let's look at Jude's statement regarding *strange flesh*:

> *Just as Sodom and Gomorrah and the cities around them, since they in the same way as these angels indulged in sexual perversion and went after strange flesh, are exhibited as an example in undergoing the punishment of eternal fire.* (Jude 1:7 NASB)

This strange desire is indicated by the Greek word *heteras* and followed by the word *sarkos*. Used together, it is literally translated as going after "different, strange, or another human body." Meaning, not a kind or type of angelic or supernatural being, but a departure from the God-designed complementary plan for sexuality.

Jude says the men of Sodom were judged for this *contrary* behavior and stand as an example of God's willingness to judge such actions in the future.

> *This interpretation is entirely in keeping with first century Jewish norms. Josephus and Philo not only condemn relations that are "contrary to nature," they explicitly understand Genesis 19 as referring to homosexual acts in the whole teaching of Scripture. (See Genesis 1:26–28; 2:21–24; Leviticus 18:1–30; Matthew 19:3–6; Mark 10:2–9.)*

As we've said throughout the book, the best interpretation of the Scriptures is the simplest. It is when we try to add to or subtract from a text that we are thinking too hard and try to make the Bible say what it is not intending. From what Jude is saying about this narrative, this text should not be so divisive.

QUESTION #4

WHY THE SUDDEN CHANGE AND REFORM IN SEXUALITY?

There are multiple reasons—a history of conservative culture in America, the speed of the information age, evolving loss of media censorship, the changing generational acceptance of homosexuality, and the secularization of the church, to name a few.

The Apple TV+ series *Visible: Out on Television*—from Emmy-nominated filmmakers Ryan White and Jessica Hargrave with executive producers Wanda Sykes and Wilson Cruz—investigates the importance of TV as an intimate medium that has shaped the American perception of the LGBTQ+ movement. The miniseries covers the painfully slow evolution of another part of the sexual revolution in modern America.

In one episode of *Visible*, Ellen DeGeneres talks about her decision to discuss her homosexuality on her television show. She said, *"I called the executive producers over to my house and I told them that I wanted to come out. It became bigger than any of us ever anticipated."*

Coming Out

The interesting question of whether to *come out* is one I hear often. The answer has a lot to do with the changing sexual revolution that is going on. When a movement or an issue becomes more accepted socially, no matter what it may be, people who believe in the movement become emboldened.

> *The evolving road of gays going public in American society is a slowly winding avenue of both pain and progress. We can see this in the pace at which change has taken place to get where we are today. And what is clear, because of this progress and pain, the church should be side by side with them in godly love.*

Remember when the *firsts* began to happen on television? Whether it was the first interracial couple, the first kiss, the first nudity, the first graphic murder scene, or the first curse word, everything else that followed came like an avalanche.

For example, take the first curse word ever said on television. In March 1965, on an episode of *My Favorite Martian*, actress Doris Packer portrays a school teacher who receives a watch at an awards ceremony. Ad-libbing, she quips, "Damn thing probably doesn't even keep time," making TV history.[67]

The first recurring gay TV character appeared in 1972 (*The Corner Bar*), but it took twenty years for TV to show the first kiss between two people of the same sex (*L.A. Law*).[68]

Not too long ago, in 2004, CBS was fined $3.6 million for an episode of *Without A Trace* that featured high school teenagers in various stages of undress taking part in an orgy.[69]

With the pace of change concerning sexuality rapidly evolving in the past two decades now, we can see how quickly gays have *come out* and become a force in culture, entertainment, and politics. Here are a few of my thoughts on why the sudden shift has taken place.

---

67. *My Favorite Martian*, "We Love You, Miss Pringle," March 28, 1965 (www.imdb.com/title/tt0654576).
68. Dan Avery, "Before 'Ellen': A Timeline Of LGBT Television," *NewNowNext*, April 27, 2017 (www.newnownext.com/gay-television-timeline/04/2017).
69. Danish Baig, "10 Memorable And Defiant Firsts In TV History," *Listverse*, December 10, 2013 (listverse.com/2013/12/10/10-memorable-and-defying-firsts-in-tv-history).

> ***The pervasive conservative mindset toward homosexuality and other sexual immoralities in culture has been replaced by a more progressive mindset.***

The church once had a great impact on society. Her strong biblical moral constitution brought a strong biblical conviction to culture. The pulpits in America were the source of prophetic direction for the nation. The influence of the church's morality on government, education, business, and entertainment was healthy and powerful. Our society depended upon this influence of biblical moral absolutes. But when the church lost its *emphasis* on these absolutes, the church ultimately lost its *influence* in society. And in the late 1990s, church membership went into a freefall.[70]

> ***A religious shift took place in America prior to 2000 that left the church and its absolutes behind.*** *This moral relativism crashed on the shore of American society and dumped all kinds of debris on the doorstep of the church. And the church lost its constitution and its voice. Society hasn't recovered from the storm of this progressive humanistic mindset in twenty-five years.*

Could it be that when the church missed the moral relativism discussion, the culture took one more step away from its conservative mindset? This began the societal journey away from the Bible and the conviction of homosexuality and other sexual immoralities as sinful. Instead of checking our feelings through moral absolutes in Scripture, we began listening to our own feelings as the new moral guide. The lack of a conservative emphasis in the church became a lack of influence in the culture.

---

70. Jeffrey M. Jones, "U.S. Church Membership Down Sharply in Past Two Decades," Gallup, April 18, 2019 (news.gallup.com/poll/248837/church-membership-down-sharply-past-two-decades.aspx).

Look at another reason for the sudden *coming out.*

> ***The pace of change resulting from the lost
> conservative mindset was staggering.*** *The exchange
> of conservative biblical truth for our own personal feelings
> became the new religion I like to call meology. It can also
> be called humanism, relativism, rationalism, and personal
> fulfillment. With this thinking came a whirlwind pace of
> change in society.*

Like it or not, our society was not comfortable with homosexuality even twenty-five years ago. The evolution has been recent. Similar to other sexuality issues, our world has had a moral framework that did not allow for sexual immorality. Until recently. No one can deny that for more than two hundred years in American history, homosexuality and other sexual immoralities were anathema. This is part of the problem. The church did not know how to react in love and truth; *it became known for everything it was against and not what it was for.*

For example, along with homosexuality, things such as nonbinary gender identity, the LGBTQ+ movement of unrestrictive labels for personal gender and sexual identity, fornication (sexual relations before marriage), gay marriage, or even bestiality were inarguably, by societal default, considered immoral or *queer* twenty-five years ago. Please understand, I am not using *queer* in a homophobic way, but in the self-expressive way it has become the popular term among those who do not fall into a binary definition of sexuality and gender. It's part of the LGBTQ+ acronym.

> *The fact I included bestiality in a sexual immorality list is
> not only offensive to some people, but also absurd. However,
> I assure you that the way we felt about homosexuality
> twenty-five years ago is the way we feel about bestiality*

> today. *"Homosexuality will never be fully accepted,"* some
> say. *But that is changing radically right before our eyes.*
> *Bestiality has now become a growing common behavior*
> *and lifestyle among young people. Like the shift in thinking*
> *regarding fornication,* **it will only be a matter of time**
> **before sex with animals will also have its cultural**
> **coming out movement.**

So, you can see the pace of cultural acceptance and change in sexuality has been a quick metamorphosis that has only taken a little more than two decades.

Here's another reason for the sudden *coming out* in the gay community.

> *There's been a loss of theology in young people and ultimately*
> *an entire generation.*
>
> *This rapid change should trigger some biblically critical*
> *thinking in us. What brought the sudden sexual revolution?*
> *Why the change in mindset? Could it be that society*
> *as a whole was wrong for many centuries? Has society*
> *never asked these questions before? Did we just find new*
> *interpretation and commentary from the Hebrew and Greek*
> *translations of the Bible on this subject?* **Has the Bible**
> **suddenly become culturally irrelevant?**

Let me give you my theory on this relatively sudden generational change and shift.

In multiple studies, including the Barna Group *Gen Z* report from February 2018, one of the most disturbing trends is the lack of theology among the vast majority of those born between 1998 and 2013. There has been a declining theological worldview in every generational set over the last eighty years. Teenagers today, Gen

Z, have a 4 percent biblical worldview, meaning only 4 percent of teenagers in America process life through a biblical lens or framework. I believe this is one of the most disturbing trends in American history.

Generational Loss

> Today's young people believe gender is still something that has to be discovered about themselves, rather than something that has divinely been given to them.
> —Whitney Tellez, youth pastor

What we are seeing in this generation is a loss of principles, a complete loss of absolutes that at one time were common default settings in our morality, such as male and female as binary gender. Today, it is customary for young people to have very few non-negotiables about sexuality or anything else. They accept gender neutrality and the nonbinary narrative. Even Gen Z teens who identify as Christians can only name half of the Ten Commandments.

The latest *coming out* wasn't because the Bible became suddenly irrelevant. Nor did we discover new definitions of Greek or Hebrew words, or unearth more Jewish history. Society has not just started asking the right questions and determined that everything we knew for centuries was wrong. The brightest minds did not come of age in the last twenty-five years.

No, this shift took place because of what I call *generational loss*. The reason for the loss of theology in a generation can be seen in a technological analogy.

Vinyl records, cassette tapes, VHS tapes, CDs, and other recordings lose their clarity over time. This may be due to wear, weather, accidents, or damage, but the *generational loss* in sound quality is real. In the same way, sexual immorality over time has gone through a process of generational loss. It became viral because of progressive individuals and movements within society who challenged a conservative culture and church that was, at the same time, moving away from a biblical worldview.

This leads me to the final reason for the *coming out* of gays in America.

> *The challenge of thinking by progressives and the moving away from truth by conservatives was the perfect storm. The church became secularized and drifted toward an emphasis on culture rather than Scripture.*

The church lost the battle for truth and became buckled under a culture that was much louder. Silence is the enemy of truth. What happened in the church was a *lack of the theology of sexuality*, an *ignorance of how to deal with the sexual revolution*, specifically homosexuality, and *the secularization of the church* being passed on to the children, *not the sacredness of the Scriptures.*

Some will say people have *come out* because they are free from the oppression of the church, and people and culture are more accepting. This is certainly true of the unchurched world, but the church world hasn't done a very good job of loving unconditionally. This is where the church must become better. I don't see proper, *loving* scriptural theology as oppressive. I see it as conviction and compassion. And when loving scriptural theology is missing, so are conviction and compassion.

Let me explain.

First, the oppression or drift many people talk about from the past cannot only be interpreted as judgment or criticism. Much of it should simply be regarded as conviction. But as humanism and *meology* have become society's moral standards, what we once called conviction is now labeled as oppression.

The church failed to hold to its historical and biblical unity in the late 1990s and splintered into factions that would begin to treat the Scriptures recklessly. Even though at the time, culture and the church were thinking almost universally toward these things, the drift began. Certainly now, the church hasn't handled its relationship with the sexual revolution very well at all.

Second, society is more accepting of the sexual revolution today because the loss of absolutes has made progressive thinking the new normal. This *meological* shift didn't just take place in society. The church, too, became increasingly secular, humanistic, and less biblical. Teachings on sexuality and morality are missing.

> *When the church lost its anchor to the Scriptures, our culture lost its mooring to absolutes. And the church no longer informed the culture, but the opposite occurred. If one generation loses its absolutes, where will the next generation get theirs?*

With this loss of scriptural integrity, the church has become without a moral constitution, ultimately losing its voice in this world to help return our society to a biblical sexuality.

As the winds of change blew around the church, the church was unable to respond with truth and grace. It was powerless to clearly speak the *truth* of Scripture to bring any correction to the cultural drift and powerless to be heard because it lost the relationship of *grace* in culture. This lack of a moral constitution and convictions spiraled into a broken relationship between Christians and culture. And the resulting response from the church to the world was judgment and oppression rather than truth and grace.

This loss of constitution and relationship in the church toward the culture made the church ineffective to an emboldened society that was pressing the envelope of thought.

Let's talk about another tough question.

QUESTION #5

IS MASTURBATION A SIN?

No...and yes.

There are two correct answers for this question. Which sounds like a compromising place to be on the issue. From a sociological and medical approach, masturbation has benefits and detriments, both physically and mentally. But from a biblical and moral sense, masturbation could involve several sin issues, including habitual addiction, pornographic material, and immoral lustful self-sex.

No doubt given all of the content in this book, I will get a lot of comments concerning this question and response. I'm okay with that. Unless we raise the temperature in the room, we may never deal directly with life's issues.

Sociological Studies

Multiple sociological sexual studies and scholarly articles indicate that 95 percent of males and 89 percent of females have used masturbation or personal self-stimulation. Studies have shown that it:

- Increases mood, stamina, sleep, and sexual desire

- Decreases the chances of contracting sexually transmitted diseases

- Can be a method of birth control for couples who practice masturbation right before sex

- Helps the development of adolescents and their sexuality

- Is a viable alternative to infidelity for married couples who may be apart from one another

- Helps couples communicate and understand what stimulates each other

> *Professional organizations such as the American Academy of Pediatrics and the American College of Obstetrics and Gynecology recognize masturbation as a normal component of child and adolescent development.*[71]

But in these same social research studies, there is a dark side to masturbation. While there may be benefits, as the psychological and medical industry says, masturbation has also increased shame, poor work performance, isolation, a tendency toward homosexuality, and pornography addiction. To be fair and comprehensive, the same research studies also found masturbation has resulted in increased feelings of guilt and fear in teenagers,[72] driven a wedge between husbands and wives, and caused sleeplessness.

Like many issues on morality—such as drinking, swearing, gambling, smoking, and others—masturbation has been proven to be amoral, or neutral, by the social studies field.

But let's look at another answer to the question of whether masturbation is a sin.

Scriptural Study

Multiple theological sexuality studies have led to a variety of viewpoints on the subject. The conversations and resulting stances on masturbation cannot necessarily be split into classic/

---

71. Cynthia L. Robbins, et al, "Prevalence, Frequency, and Associations of Masturbation With Partnered Sexual Behaviors Among US Adolescents," *Archives of Pediatrics & Adolescent Medicine*, December 2011 (jamanetwork.com/journals/jamapediatrics/fullarticle/1107656).
72. Jannine Ray and Shelby Afflerbach, "Sexual Education and Attitudes toward Masturbation," *Journal of Undergraduate Research at Minnesota State University*, 2014, Vol. 14, Article 8 (cornerstone.lib.mnsu.edu/cgi/viewcontent.cgi?article=1052&context=jur).

conservative or contemporary/progressive frameworks. Both have a stated theological foundation. Some Christian authors have supported a use of masturbation without shame or guilt that does not involve pornography, idolatry, immorality, or lust. The debate is an interesting one.

James Dobson, the founder of Focus on the Family, and other conservatives have stressed the use of masturbation without pornography as a positive thing. The Catholic Church calls it "objectively disordered or intrinsically evil" when done outside the state of marriage.[73]

> So, to answer this question is to solve two dilemmas. Do we accept masturbation without pornography or immorality in mind? Do we reject masturbation as lust and self-sex? It is, then, trying to determine a theology of sexuality that would allow masturbation (within or outside of the context of marriage) by determining it is not lust or self-sex, and by determining it is not accompanied by pornography or immorality.

Adults or Youth

I can't find anyone to tell me this is right or wrong. I feel like I know if I'm doing something sinful. And this is one of those issues I wish I knew was right or wrong.

—Jacque, age 20

Interestingly, the response to the question can change depending on who is asking it.

---

73. "Masturbation," Catholic Education Resource Center (www.catholiceducation.org/en/marriage-and-family/sexuality/masturbation.html).

For example, if a married man or woman is asking the question regarding masturbation between times of having sex with their spouse, it might be easier to answer. Sickness, pregnancy, children, or travel may cause the regular sex life between a husband and wife to be sporadic. I will say, to me, the greater problem answering this question within marriage is how the husband and wife approach their sexual relationship and fulfill each other's needs. I think masturbation would be less of an issue in a healthy marriage where both spouses are seeking to meet each other's spiritual, emotional, and physical needs.

However, on the other end of the spectrum, for someone like Jacque, who is a spiritual leader in her youth group, there is a real desire to have a clear answer on this topic. I've heard this question asked by many teenagers who are mature spiritually and simply want to know if masturbation is wrong when no pornography or immoral thoughts are involved. Teenagers say using masturbation without pornography and immorality in mind has helped them to avoid sexual sins and relieve the sexual pressure from an immoral society.

Let's answer the question in four parts.

First, the scriptural resolution on the subject. (See Genesis 38; Matthew 5:28; Philippians 4:8–9; 1 Peter 4:1–3; James 1:12–16; 1 Thessalonians 4:3–5; Colossians 3:5.)

Some will point to the story of Onan in Genesis 38 as a prohibition and judgment against masturbation. Here, however, Onan was judged not because he spilled his seed on the ground, but because he was disobedient and did not impregnate Tamar to carry on the family name. These other passages of Scripture deal with immorality and selfish ambition; they do not deal directly with masturbation without pornography or immorality attached. And so, if we cannot find a specific statement from God against an action, it is unfair—and, frankly, poor hermeneutics and exegesis—to place upon someone a burden or shame that is unscriptural. Similar to the other topics in this book. (See Galatians 1; 1 Peter 4.)

However, if we look at these texts from the standpoint of a theology of sex and determine that masturbation is lust and self-sex outside of marriage, it would be considered sexual immorality like many other prohibited acts. Scripture is not clear that masturbation without pornography or immorality is prohibited and thus a sin. So what do we do?

Masturbation could actually be a way to release the natural buildup of semen for men or erotic feelings for women, keeping them from falling into lustful temptations. On the other hand, if masturbation is done with pornography or immorality in mind, whether within a marriage or not, it would be sexual sin.

> *Looking at these texts, we see the strong command to possess our vessels—our bodies—with honor, purity, and godliness, not with selfish ambition, lust, or immorality. This is where each person must answer for themselves whether masturbation is lustful self-sex and thus unclean or immoral. I believe the scriptural key in answer to this question is more about lust than it is about masturbation.*

Second, **the physiological resolution on the subject.** When I was younger, I remember one youth pastor saying that if we masturbated, we would go blind, lose our fertility, and end up in hell. Yep. Well, it worked. I never looked at pornography growing up, partly because it was difficult to find, but mostly because of convictions placed into my life early—like my youth pastor's words! I can say that in all of my teenage and young adult years, I had zero addiction to pornography or masturbation. I was afraid of them both.

Let me give you some practical thoughts on what I have learned and often share with teens I have counseled over the years on the topic of masturbation:

1. *Words* – words are faith and daily discipline that lead to purity. Speaking *"I will not"* in the moment of temptation is powerful. Our words determine our response to temptation, lust, and pornography daily and lead us to purity wins.

2. *Wins* – wins are when you do not fall to the temptation of masturbation or any sexual immorality through lust and pornography. Building on wins by writing them down or sharing them with a friend is a powerful deterrent and makes it easier to win the next time.

3. *Worship* – worship at the point of temptation. There may be nothing more able to change the setting than worship. I have told many students to create a playlist you can turn to immediately at the point of temptation.

4. *Wired* – we are wired by God. God has built into each of us a biological, natural, and timely orgasmic release of semen for men and erotic feelings for women. That natural regular orgasm may occur every several days or several weeks, depending on the person.

This physical and natural function of orgasmic relief is God's way out of persistent societal pressure for you. The *wet dreams* or *hot flashes* are the best natural release of physical and emotional sexual buildup in our bodies. They are not selfish, shameful, or sinful. It is our responsibility to use these four practical thoughts to win first, but God's physiology is a huge assist.

Third, the sexual resolution on the subject. It has been a long-time myth that sexuality is a dirty and unclean thing. *It is not; it's a God-given gift.* As related directly to the question, masturbation itself will not cause blindness or sterility or drag you to hell. However, with this question, we have a perfect example where sexuality can become dirty or unclean, depending upon our use of it.

> *So, what is critical in my response to answering the question*
> *is what may accompany the act of masturbation—such*
> *as pornography, mental foreplay with someone in mind,*
> *dishonor to God or my body, or an uncontrollable habit. These*
> *sexual prohibitions are forbidden and unclean immoralities,*
> *and if they accompany masturbation, it would miss the mark.*

To be clear, any kind of transient or intermittent masturbation would be wrong if it is accompanied by these lustful prohibitions. Throughout the day, variables occur that come against our purity and build up sexual tension in our life. But remember, there are several ways to deal with this as we have shown in the practical area above. Maybe another way of dealing with this tension is through masturbation done within God's physiological assist and not in our own lusts. Otherwise, it becomes habitual self-sex.

Finally, the practical resolution on the subject. I believe the direct answer to this question is to wait for your body's natural, God-given release moment, and, *if needed,* to use masturbation at that time. If you are able to flee immorality and be disciplined *up until that moment*, there will be no pornography or immorality involved. If you're able to separate immorality from the act, masturbation at the time of your body's natural orgasm can be a timely release of powerful physical and emotional feelings.

> *With that said, if we are not disciplined and we allow the*
> *shameful habit of pornography and lust to control our life,*
> *masturbation will become our master and, ultimately, we*
> *will miss the mark. Do not let masturbation become a part of*
> *the act of pornography or immorality.*

Paul called us to flee immorality and not be mastered by it. (See 1 Corinthians 6:18.) That makes each person responsible for managing lust, relationships, pornography, and sensual pleasure in moments of temptation in their life. What is clear in this Scripture is that nothing, including masturbation, should ever become your master, compulsive, or habit-forming and a lustful act.

This is why it is so critical to have a healthy discussion on sexuality at an early age in the home. You will find more help in chapter five. Adolescents growing into their sexuality need spiritual leaders who will help them with this conversation if it is not being done at home.

QUESTION #6

AS A WOMAN WITH LEADERSHIP GIFTS AND A DESIRE TO SERVE THE CHURCH, DOES GOD, AND THE SCRIPTURES, HAVE A PLACE FOR ME?

Yes.

One of the things that often happens in a theological argument that's really unfair is using the Bible to prove one's own point, or taking a single Scripture and trying to define what the Bible is saying about an issue. We cannot take the Scriptures—or anything else, for that matter—out of context. The theological principle here is called *proof-texting*, or trying to prove something from a single passage, line, or phrase from a document.

Theopedia defines *proof-texting* as "the method by which a person appeals to a biblical text to prove or justify a theological position without regard for the context of the passage they are citing."[74]

Sure, there are the classic, humorous examples of proof-texting, like when you are praying for direction to consider a family move, open your Bible, and read Psalm 139:8 (NASB): *"If I make my bed in Sheol* [the place of the dead], *behold, You are there."* That doesn't mean we

---

74. www.theopedia.com/proof-texting.

have to move to hell. Actually, while writing this chapter, I asked Siri where hell was located and was told it was 497 miles away from Minneapolis—Hell, Michigan.

Or maybe you have heard of the example of wanting to hear from God on direction for your life, so you open up the Bible and point to a text. In doing this, you read, *"Judas threw the silver coins into the Temple and left. Then he went out and hung himself"* (Matthew 27:5). Not excited about that text, you try it again. You open to Luke 10 and read, *"Go and do the same"* (verse 37). Of course, this sounds silly, but this is exactly what we are doing when we take Scripture out of context.

> *When it comes to the question about the role of women in the church, there may not be any other topic in culture that gets cheapened so often by proof-texting. It is something that must be dealt with honestly on both sides of the theological aisle for any topic of discussion, especially this question of equality and women in ministry.*

Textual Proof of Equality

When it comes to feminism and equality, we must be scripturally accurate and understand the intent of the biblical writers. It can be easy to proof-text the Bible's warnings and cautions on this subject without grasping the Scripture's message or the entire biblical record.

This question and discussion is as much about the place of women in ministry as it is about human equality. At first glance, there are verses that directly prohibit women leading men and seemingly place a fence or ceiling around women in leadership. But a thorough reading of the specific setting of these words—and the overall context of the Bible—gives us a much clearer view on how God feels about women in leadership and ministry. Furthermore, reading the whole Bible gives a more complete picture of human equality and partiality.

For example, look at these verses as they relate to feminism and equality:

> So God created human beings, making them to be like himself. He
> created them male and female. (Genesis 1:27 GNT)

What I find remarkable in the Bible is the extent to which God is likened to both male and female characteristics and traits. This is the powerful emphasis of God in the sense of *anthropomorphism*, describing God with human attributes. But it's also interesting how humankind is likened to God. This gives us a beautiful inclusive relationship of Creator and created.

> He told the Woman: "I'll multiply your pains in childbirth; you'll
> give birth to your babies in pain. You'll want to please your hus-
> band, but he'll lord it over you." He told the Man: "Because you
> listened to your wife and ate from the tree that I commanded you
> not to eat from, 'Don't eat from this tree,' the very ground is cursed
> because of you; getting food from the ground will be as painful as
> having babies is for your wife; you'll be working in pain all your life
> long. The ground will sprout thorns and weeds, you'll get your food
> the hard way, planting and tilling and harvesting, sweating in the
> fields from dawn to dusk, until you return to that ground yourself,
> dead and buried; you started out as dirt, you'll end up dirt."
> (Genesis 3:16–19)

Just prior to this, God placed curses on Satan. (See verses 14–15.) *Then God addressed both the man and the woman*, telling them both of their future limitations. This is clearly God's correction to man and woman equally. Nobody can argue otherwise.

> This is the book of the generations of Adam. On the day when God
> created man, He made him in the likeness of God. He created them

male and female, and He blessed them and named them "man-
kind" [Adam] on the day when they were created.

(Genesis 5:1–2 NASB)

As God first created mankind, He called *their* name Adam. It wasn't
until God created a helpmate for Adam that God divided out of the
Adam (mankind) a female so they could have the compatibility
and purpose of cocreating together. The woman (Eve), as she would
ultimately be called, was created not from Adam's head, to rule over
him, nor was Eve created from Adam's foot, to be trampled by him.
No. The woman Eve was created from Adam's side, so they could be
held together in unison as the perfect picture of God's image. This is
the equality and the value of woman.

Now, look at these verses as they relate to human equality:

I will pour out my Spirit on every kind of people: your sons will
prophesy, also your daughters....I'll even pour out my Spirit on the
servants, men and women both.   (Joel 2:28–29)

Even in the Old Testament, countless stories are told of women
whom God used greatly for His kingdom—women such as Hagar,
Tamar, Miriam, Rahab, Esther, and more. When it comes to ministry
or the works of the Spirit, it is clear God has appointed both women
and men for His work. Throughout the Scriptures and church history,
there are multiple examples of women in ministry used by God as
evidence of His overwhelming approval.

In Christ's family there can be no division into Jew and non-Jew,
slave and free, male and female. Among us you are all equal.

(Galatians 3:28)

At that time, the church in Galatia was divided and fighting among
themselves. Paul stressed that they were all one and should be

treating each other without partiality. The point he was making was not about the devaluing of race or gender in the role of the church. Paul was emphasizing that we should all be treating each other with equal respect and honor. Again, it is important for us to read the Scriptures in context.

> *My friends, as believers in our Lord Jesus Christ, the Lord of glory, you must never treat people in different ways according to their outward appearance....If you treat people according to their outward appearance, you are guilty of sin.* (James 2:1, 9 GNT)

What is very clear in Scripture is the comprehensive argument for the equality of humankind. Even in the uniqueness of our gender, race, or role in life, there is a divine mandate for respect, value, and honor for all of humanity, regardless of our sex. *If we do not love unconditionally, we have missed the mark.*

> *I do not allow a woman to teach or to exercise authority over a man, but to remain quiet.* (1 Timothy 2:12 NASB)

Paul's words here and in similar passages referred to the individual behavior of those women who were being insubordinate at the time. This is why in the purist Greek renderings, Paul is actually placing a *timely prohibition* upon insubordinate behavior and not making a blanket statement about women in leadership for all time. In fact, Paul mentions specific women in ministry with him, including Phoebe and Priscilla. (See Romans 16.)

Here is a great commentary on the whole of Scripture and a woman's role in ministry:

> There are only two passages in the entire New Testament that might seem to contain a prohibition against the ministry of women (1 Corinthians 14:34 and 1 Timothy 2:12). Since these

must be placed alongside Paul's other statements and practices, they can hardly be absolute, unequivocal prohibitions of the ministry of women. Instead, they seem to be dealing with specific, local problems that needed correction. Therefore, Paul's consistent affirmation of ministering women among his churches must be seen as his true perspective, rather than the apparent prohibitions of these two passages, themselves subject to conflicting interpretation.[75]

All of these texts simply and clearly prove the equality of the two genders, the many races, and the titles and roles of humanity at the creation and relationship level.

Here is how I see equality. There isn't confusion in the creation account; there is great clarity. God created us in His image as human and He completed us by creating us with unique human traits as male and female to complement one another. Additionally, the whole of Scripture should be read as supporting the blessing and the call of God upon the lives of *all flesh, both sons and daughters.*

A FRESH LOOK AT THE BEGINNING

We started this book with one of the iconic passages of Scripture. In First Corinthians chapter 13, Paul is addressing the people of Corinth on their love of gifts and talents. After all, Corinth was quite a city and had a reputation for being spectacular in setting, with gifted, talented people. Paul even said at the beginning of his letter to them in chapter one that the people did not fall short in their gifts.

Much like America today.

Paul is dealing with love, the characteristic trait of our faith as Christians. After listing all kinds of spectacular gifts in the first

---

75. "The Role of Women in Ministry (Adopted by the General Presbytery in session August 9-11, 2010)" (ag.org/Beliefs/Position-Papers/The-Role-of-Women-in-Ministry).

part of chapter 13, Paul says that if we do not have love, it profits us nothing. He goes on to describe love in the middle part of the chapter with a fantastic display of love in colorful language. And then, at the end of this chapter, he talks about a rite of passage or a coming of age. Look at these words in verse 11 (GNT):

> *When I was a child, my speech, feelings, and thinking were all those of a child; now that I am an adult, I have no more use for childish ways.*

Wow. Did you catch that? At some point in our life, we have to recognize that our growth and discipleship in Christianity is not about speaking in tongues, prophecy, understanding mysteries and knowledge, having faith to do miracles, or even giving to the poor. *Our growth in Christianity and discipleship is about love.* Everything else is secondary and supplemental. Love is primary. And so we end with love.

Because I never want to win an argument and lose a relationship.

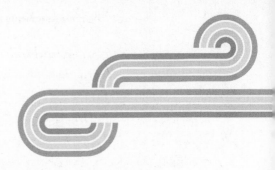

If I speak with human eloquence and angelic ecstasy but don't love,

I'm nothing but the creaking of a rusty gate.

If I speak God's Word with power, revealing all his mysteries and making everything plain as day, and if I have faith that says to a mountain, "Jump," and it jumps,

but I don't love, I'm nothing.

If I give everything I own to the poor and even go to the stake to be burned as a martyr, but I don't love, I've gotten nowhere. So, no matter what I say, what I believe, and what I do,

I'm bankrupt without love.

Love never gives up.
Love cares more for others than for self.
Love doesn't want what it doesn't have.
Love doesn't strut,
Doesn't have a swelled head,
Doesn't force itself on others,
Isn't always "me first,"
Doesn't fly off the handle,
Doesn't keep score of the sins of others,
Doesn't revel when others grovel,
Takes pleasure in the flowering of truth,
Puts up with anything,
Trusts God always,
Always looks for the best,

Never looks back,
But keeps going to the end.

*Love never dies. Inspired speech will be over some day; praying
in tongues will end; understanding will reach its limit. We know
only a portion of the truth, and what we say about God is always
incomplete. But when the Complete arrives, our incompletes will
be canceled.*

*When I was an infant at my mother's breast, I gurgled and cooed
like any infant. When I grew up, I left those infant ways for good.*

*We don't yet see things clearly. We're squinting in a fog, peering
through a mist. But it won't be long before the weather clears and
the sun shines bright! We'll see it all then, see it all as clearly as
God sees us, knowing him directly just as he knows us!*

*But for right now, until that completeness, we have three things
to do to lead us toward that consummation: Trust steadily in God,
hope unswervingly, love extravagantly.*

And the best of the three is love.

—1 Corinthians 13

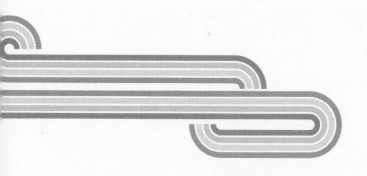

ABOUT THE AUTHOR

Jeff Grenell is a nationally recognized youth ministry veteran who inspires youth leaders across denominations.

After four decades in youth leadership, Jeff and his late wife, Jane, founded ythology to both reach and teach youth and train youth leaders to prepare the next generations to lead in the church and the world. Jeff is also a youth specialist at North Central University's Church Leadership School.

A former youth pastor at churches in Michigan, Indiana, and Ohio, he has traveled around the world to teach youth ministry and development at churches, conventions, universities, and leadership training conferences.

Jeff attended Evangel University in Springfield, Missouri, where he received his B.A. in Communications and Theology and his M.A. in Organizational Leadership. Jeff makes his home in Minneapolis and has coached basketball and soccer. He has three adult children and a growing number of grandchildren.